LIVING DINOSAURS
AND OTHER REPTILES

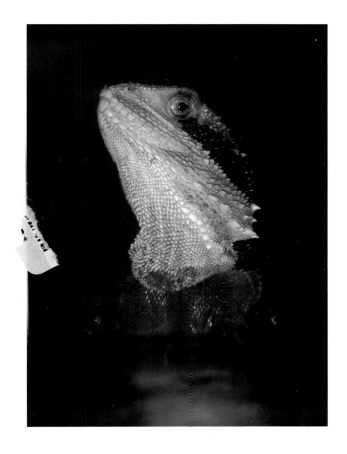

First published in the
United Kingdom in 2009 by:
Evans Mitchell Books
The Old Forge, Forge Mews
16 Church Street
Rickmansworth
Hertfordshire WD3 1DH
United Kingdom
www.embooks.co.uk

Design by:
Darren Westlake
TU ink Ltd, London
www.tuink.co.uk

The title of this book was conceived by
Ben Evans – when aged 9

British Library Cataloguing in Publication Data.
A CIP record of this book is available
on request from the British Library.

ISBN: 978-1-901268-36-2

Printed in China

LIVING
DINOSAURS
AND OTHER REPTILES

HEATHER ANGEL

Evans Mitchell Books

Contents

Introduction

The way in which living reptiles are related to prehistoric reptiles is constantly being revised, as more and earlier fossils are unearthed and dating becomes more sophisticated. The earliest reptiles, descendents of ancient amphibian-like creatures, appeared about 300 million years ago (mya). These ancestral reptiles were able to invade land by developing a waterproof skin and laying shelled eggs in which their young could develop on land. Together with the dinosaurs and the pterosaurs (the first flying reptiles, often known as pterodactyls), crocodilians (modern crocodiles and alligators) and birds have evolved from an ancestral group known as the Archosauria or Ruling Reptiles.

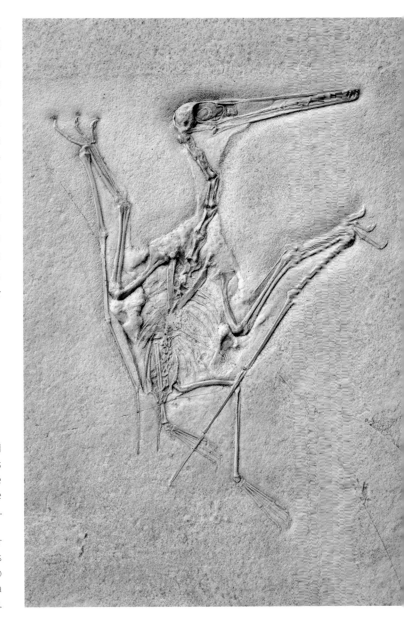

Right: Dating back to the Jurassic, this pterodactyl (*Pterodactylus kochi*) had a wing span of 46 centimetres (1.5 feet) supported by the elongated fourth digit on the hand. Prey was captured by this carnivorous flying reptile in the long, pointed beak armed with many small teeth.

Opposite: Australia's largest lizard, the perentie or gigantic lace lizard (*Varanus giganteus*) reaches 2.5 metres (eight feet) in length and is a top predator. Once hunted by Aboriginals, it has a reticulated pattern of black lines and flecks.

Dinosaurs began to appear about 230 mya; they were so successful they roamed and ruled our Earth as the dominant vertebrates for 160 million years. It was the anatomist Sir Richard Owen who coined the word 'dinosaur' in 1841, derived from the Greek words meaning 'terrible lizard'; although in fact, they were not true lizards.

Then, 65 mya, at the end of the Cretaceous, dinosaurs were wiped off the Earth. The most plausible cause was a catastrophic environmental change as a result of a vast iridium-rich asteroid colliding with the Earth to create a crater at Chicxulub on Mexico's Yucatan Peninsula. The massive dust clouds that formed as a result of the impact would have blocked out the sun, killing off vegetation; thereby causing the death of herbivorous dinosaurs followed by the carnivorous species.

Amongst the four living groups of reptiles (Crocodylia, Rhynchocephalia, Squamata and Testudines) that survived this apocalyptic event, only one – the Crocodylia (alligators, crocodiles, caiman and the gharial) – is closely related to dinosaurs. The Rhynchocephalia (tuatara) are often referred to as living dinosaurs because their external appearance has changed little over 200 million years; but recent research has found their DNA has evolved quite rapidly. The Squamata (lizards, worm lizards and snakes) evolved from another ancestral group known as the Lepidosauria. While the exact origin of the Testudines (turtles and tortoises) remains a mystery as the skull structure varies between species.

Above: The Indian gharial or gavial (*Gavialis gangeticus*) is the sole living species of gavialoids, and has a long slender snout; these reptiles are hauled out on a sand bar in the Chambal River, India.

Opposite: Giant tortoises (*Geochelone elephantopus vandenburghi*) wallow in temporary pools on the floor of Alcedo Crater on Isabela, Galápagos.

After the dinosaurs died out, an array of ecological niches became available for other animals to exploit without having to compete with the dinosaurs. Although the reptiles we know today are not directly descended from dinosaurs, some share a common ancestor. Like the dinosaurs, they have exploited various types of feeding strategies that embrace carnivores, herbivores, omnivores and scavengers.

The scope of *Wildlife Monographs – Living Dinosaurs and other reptiles* makes it impossible to cover more than a small selection of modern reptiles. These have been chosen for the fascinating stories associated with them or the cunning means they have developed to lure and capture their prey, to fend off predators and simply to survive. Some of these are thought to parallel those of the dinosaurs and, indeed, are portrayed by film directors as being typical of true dinosaurs.

Above: After feeding in the cold sea, marine iguanas (*Amblyrhynchus cristatus*) bask at Punta Espiñosa in the Galápagos.

Opposite: The male Yemen chameleon (*Chamaeleo calyptratus*) has a large casque on the head.

Aquatic snappers

Crocodiles and alligators are known as crocodilians and our modern species have similar features to the first crocodile-like ancestors that appeared around 240 mya. All have an elongated snout with snapping jaws, a stream-lined body with tough protective scales and a powerful muscular tail. Present day crocodilians, the giants amongst the reptiles, are the top predators of tropical and subtropical wetlands and can be found in North and South America, Africa, Asia and Australia.

Twenty-three distinct species are placed in three major groups: true crocodiles (thirteen species), the alligators and caimans (eight species) and the gharial (*Gavialis gangeticus*). Experts cannot agree on where to place the false gharial (*Tomistoma schlegelii*); some group it with the gharial, others with the true crocodiles.

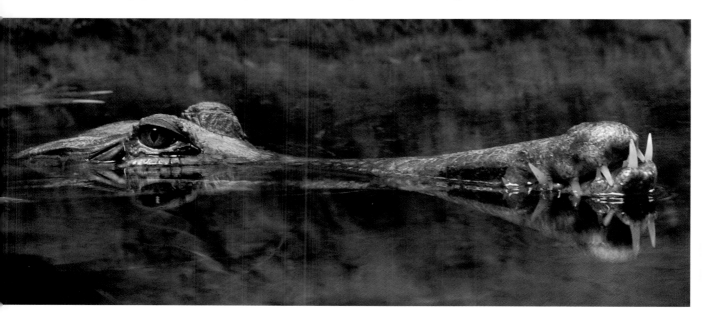

Above: Like the gharial, the false or Malayan gharial is a fish-eating freshwater reptile with slender jaws. It lives in the rainforest fringes within Malaysia, West Borneo, Java and Sumatra.

Opposite: A saltwater crocodile or saltie can use its powerful tail to propel itself right out of the water towards an unsuspecting victim.

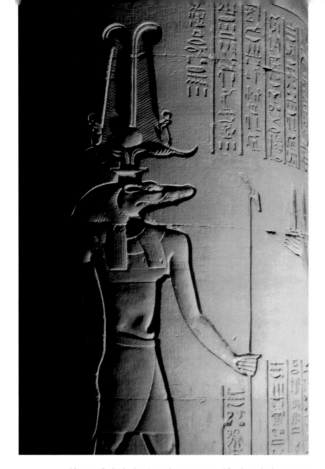

Above: Sobek depicted as a crocodile-headed man at the Kom Ombo Temple beside the River Nile in Egypt.
Photo by iStockphoto

Crocodilians have intrigued and fascinated mankind since the time of the ancient Egyptians who worshipped the crocodile-headed god, Sobek. Egyptians in the vicinity of the River Nile believed that if they prayed to Sobek, he would protect them from Nile crocodile (*Crocodylus niloticus*) attacks. Within Sobek's temple in Arsinoe (named Crocodilopolis or 'Crocodile City' by the Greeks) sacred crocodiles covered with jewellery were kept in a pool. Mummified crocodiles have even been found in Egyptian sacred tombs. Crocodile feeding shows at the Kom Ombo Temple, in Ombos on the River Nile, were popular with the Greeks and the Romans. Many tribes in Central and South America, where one caiman and two species of crocodiles occur, also worship crocodilian gods.

The recent discovery of *Isisfordia* (98-95 mya), the world's most primitive crocodilian in west Queensland – 20 million years older than the first fossil records of alligators and 30 million years before the first modern crocodiles – may mean that modern crocodiles originated in the

ancient continent of Gondwana. Alligators and caimans have broad snouts whereas crocodiles have more slender snouts. The large fourth tooth in the lower jaw of crocodiles is clearly visible even when the mouth is shut, but is hidden in alligators as it fits into a socket in the upper jaw.

Top: Saltwater crocodiles are normally highly territorial, but using infra red cameras at night, a BBC film crew managed to film over 40 salties feasting on mullet migrating up the Mary River in Australia. This animal with an unpigmented head swims at the surface of the Adelaide River.

Above: As a saltwater crocodile rests on the muddy bank of the Adelaide River in Australia, with its mouth closed, the fourth tooth in the lower jaw is clearly exposed.

Left: A crocodile basks beside the Chambal River in India.

The biggest – and most feared – of all the crocodilians is the saltwater or estuarine crocodile (*Crocodylus porosus*), found in India, south-east Asia and New Guinea as well as the northern part of Australia, where it is known affectionately as the 'saltie'. This croc lives mainly in freshwater rivers, lakes and

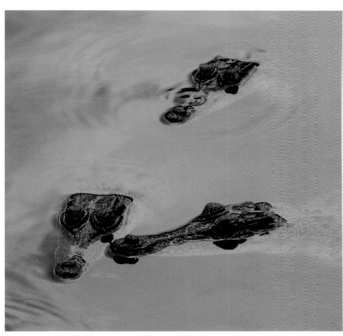

Top: All crocodilians, such as these saltwater crocodiles, can lie concealed beneath the water with just their ears, eyes and snout visible above the surface; ready to ambush any prey that ventures too close.

Left: When the palatal valve at the back of the throat is closed, the mouth can be opened underwater without water passing down the throat. Saltwater crocodile jaws snap together with a massive bite force of around 30,000 kilograms per square metre (3,000 pounds per square inch) which makes light work of crushing a turtle shell.

estuaries but some have been found 1,000 kilometres (620 miles) at sea, with barnacles attached to their bodies. On average males grow up to six metres (19.5 feet) long, with females about half the length. But this is small fry compared with the 12 metres (39 feet) long 'Supercroc' *Sarcosuchus* unearthed in the Sahara Desert in Africa, with a massive skull that had an overhanging jaw. The Supercroc lived during the Cretaceous (110 mya) when this part of Africa was dotted with lakes and rivers. It is probable, like modern crocodiles, it lay in wait for prey – which could have included dinosaurs – coming to drink.

Above: This five metres (16 feet) long saltwater crocodile belly-crawled out of the Adelaide River to rest beneath mangroves.

Crocodilians move over land and through water. On land, crocodilians move either by belly sliding or, if their legs are strong enough, by raising their body right off the ground, to walk and even to run. When space is visible between a crocodile's belly and the ground, this is known as the high walk. The Australian freshwater crocodile (*Crocodylus johnstoni*) known locally as the 'freshie', reaches up to three metres (ten feet) in length and can gallop over land at up to 18 kilometres per hour (11 miles per hour) when running downhill.

Like monitors, crocodilians make themselves more stream-lined when they swim by holding their limbs against their body; spreading them out to assist in braking when they want to stop. Their powerful tail propels them rapidly through water and large crocodiles – including the saltwater crocodile – use it to launch themselves vertically out of the water in a tail walk. With split second timing, using all three senses – smell, sight and sound – a saltie suddenly emerges from nowhere to pluck a hapless fruit bat roosting on a riverside tree overhanging water or a bird above water. Even young saltwater crocodiles will leap to catch less ambitious prey such as dragonflies.

Above: An Australian freshwater crocodile or freshie, has a slender snout and reaches about half the size of a saltie.

Below: When a crocodile submerges a third transparent eyelid — known as the nictitating membrane — moves across the eye giving it a milky appearance with the pupil still visible behind. A triangular skin flap covers the ear behind each eye.

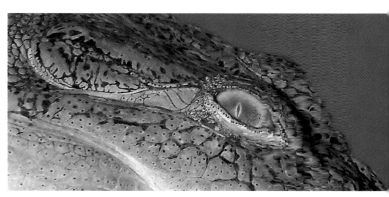

Above: One of some 2,000 saltwater crocodiles that live in the Adelaide River leaps vertically out of water using its muscular tail to catch food above the water.

Below: As an immature saltwater crocodile swims underwater, the limbs are pressed alongside the body.

Above: What is not seen: virtually the whole body of a crocodilian lies hidden underwater when it rises up to the surface, and this one is just a hatchling!

Unlike birds and mammals, crocodilians do not have to feed on a regular basis and when not active can go without food for many weeks. They capture their prey either by hunting or lying in wait. Moving prey, such as prawns and crabs in amongst tidal mangroves, attracts hatchling saltwater crocodiles. With the nostrils placed at the end of the snout, a crocodile cannot push its mouth into the mud to pick up a crab or remains of carrion. Instead, the head is turned to one side so the teeth at the side of the jaw can grasp food on land.

Adult saltwater crocodiles feed on magpie geese (*Anseranas semipalmata*) and other wetland birds, fish and freshwater turtles in billabongs and swamps; plus a host of mammals, including fruit bats, wallabies, dingoes, domestic dogs and even feral pigs – are all potential prey when they are within striking distance. The largest crocodiles are prepared to exert a major effort to bring down even more ambitious prey including cattle, horses and water buffalo.

Nile crocodiles lie in wait at the water's edge waiting for animals to come and drink or where game animals cross African rivers on their annual migration. The water suddenly explodes when a Nile crocodile leaps out of the water to latch its powerful jaws onto its prey. If an animal continues to struggle, the crocodile keeps its jaws clamped tight, making repeated rolls by rotating its body in the water until the prey gives up the fight. By cutting down the blood flow to the lungs crocodiles are able to remain underwater for hours. Hunks of flesh are torn off large prey by more body rolls, but the crocodile has to surface to feed, otherwise it would drown.

Top: A Nile crocodile seizes a gazelle when it came to a river to drink in the Masai Mara, Kenya.
Photo by blickwinkel/Alamy

Above: Paws and jaws: it is unusual to have two apex predators in such close proximity. When the leopard (*Panthera pardus*) emerged at night to poach bait put out to attract Nile crocodiles at Samburu in Kenya, it was seen off by a crocodile.

21

Larger crocodiles swallow stones, which function as ballast, as well as aiding the rapid digestion of food together with highly acidic enzymes in the stomach. Food not eaten may be stashed underwater for later, although a host of small aquatic animals will take advantage of an unexpected bounty. Crocodilians do not feed on cold days because the digestive enzymes in the stomach fail to work at low temperatures.

The optimum temperature for crocodilians is 30-33°C (86-91°F). Being cold-blooded, crocodiles and alligators control their body temperature by moving in and out of water onto land. American alligators (*Alligator mississippiensis*) move out of water to bask on land in the morning and later in the day return to the water; whereas salties adopt the reverse migration. They spend more of the day submerged and then emerge on land at night when the temperature drops.

Above: Crocodilians, such as this Nile crocodile, rest with their jaws agape to cool the brain whilst the rest of the body warms up.

Right: The American alligator is the most northerly living crocodilian; here it basks at the water's edge in Okefenokee swamp, USA.

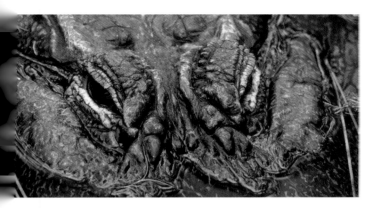

Left: American alligator eyes emerge from Okefenokee swamp in Georgia.

Distribution of saltwater crocodile
(*Crocodylus porosus*).

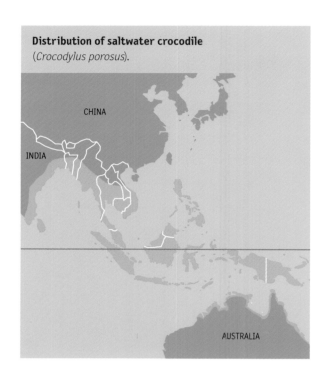

Distribution of American crocodile
(*Crocodylus acutus*).

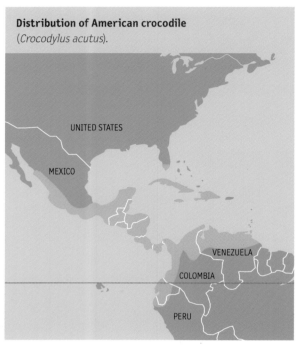

Distribution of Nile crocodile
(*Crocodylus niloticus*).

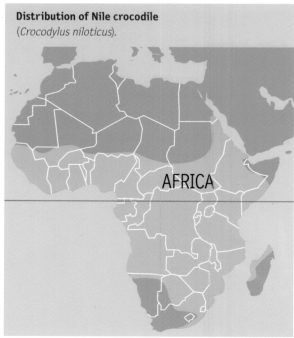

Distribution of American alligator
(*Alligator mississippiensis*).

Above: Yacaré caiman attack a dead capybara (*Hydrochaeris nydrochaeris*) in the Pantanal, Brazil

Right: Yacaré caiman hauled out beside pool in the dry season, Pantanal, Brazil

The American crocodile (*Crocodylus acutus*) extends from the northern coastline of South America, up through Central America, the Caribbean islands, to the southern tip of Florida. With males reaching up to five metres (three feet) in length, this crocodile frequents both estuaries and mangrove swamps as well as freshwater habitats.

Caimans are widespread throughout Central and South America. As pools shrink within Brazil's Pantanal, they become ringed with yacaré caiman (*Caiman yacare*) hauled out on the bank, facing towards the water so they can rapidly submerge. When water levels drop very low, caimans in South America and freshwater crocodiles in Australia hibernate in the mud.

Male Nile crocodiles mate with as many as 20 different females; whereas the territorial saltwater crocodile mates with only a few females. A mated female crocodilian lays her eggs either in a hole she excavates in sand or in a nest mound, which she builds from aquatic plants. Instead of a male or female chromosome determining the sex of crocodilians, sex is controlled by the incubation time and the temperature at which the eggs are incubated.

Above: A Nile crocodile hatchling emerges from the egg shell.
Photo by Martin Harvey/Alamy

A slow development at under 30°C (86°F) produces females; 31-33°C (88-91°F) produces mostly males and above 33°C (91°F) males in some species and females in others. The female stays near the nest until the baby crocodilians or hatchlings call from inside the egg. The female responds to their noises and starts to excavate the nest as the young begin to emerge using an egg tooth at the end of their snout to break through the egg shell. It is then that the jaws, normally associated with inflicting such brute force to kill its prey, gently carry one or two hatchlings, laid across the teeth of the lower jaw, down to the water's edge.

Many reasons contribute to the failure of eggs to hatch; infertility, flooding of nests, overheating and predation. Goannas raid nests of the saltwater crocodile in Australia and tegus will eat caiman eggs in South America.

The saltwater crocodile and the Nile crocodile are both known to attack and kill humans; the latter probably causes more human deaths than any other crocodilian – especially in the dry season where the water supply is shared by humans and crocodiles. The American alligator also causes human fatalities but it is more likely to eat domestic cats and dogs. The Indian mugger or marsh crocodile (*Crocodylus paiustris*) will kill humans in defence of its territory or to protect the young. Human remains and jewellery found in gharial stomachs would suggest they attack humans, but the most likely explanation is that the reptiles scavenge on cremated bodies dispatched into rivers.

Above: The Indian mugger or marsh crocodile basks in India t has the broadest snout of any crocodile – more typical of an alligate

Below: A baby American alligator basks on water lettuce (*Pistia stratiotes*) in Corkscrew swamp, Florida, JSA.

The saltwater crocodile population has increased in Australia since hunting bans were imposed in the northern states by the early 1970's, which has led to an increase in the number of human fatalities. Curiously, instead of deterring tourists, stories of these fatalities in the press attract more people – especially from Europe – to the notorious locations. When floods occur in urban areas there is a real risk of crocodiles invading towns and attacking people and dogs in flooded streets.

The gharial, the world's oldest crocodilian, belongs to an ancient lineage that dates back some 250 mya and is now facing extinction

in the wild. Once widespread in rivers throughout India and Pakistan, loss of habitat – notably from river pollution – has reduced its range to fragmented populations in four tributaries of the Ganges River; the Chambal, Girwa and Son Rivers in India and the Rapti-Narayani River in Nepal.

Above: Indian gharials hauled out on a sand bar in the Chambal River where they were introduced from captive breeding stock. When swimming, the long slender snout offers least resistance, while the elongated tail scutes increase the area and hence the power.

Above: Replica of an open gharial skull showing the many interlocking teeth which efficiently secure slippery fish. This reptile, which is considered sacred by Hindus, is now endangered.

Opposite: In shallow water the saltwater crocodile can stand with the tail and hind feet forming a tripod support, reminiscent of some dinosaurs.

Gharials can reach seven metres (23 feet) in length and have the narrowest snout of all crocodilians. Unlike crocodiles, the gharial is unable to raise its body off the ground in a high walk and moves solely by sliding on its belly. Slender jaws, equipped with a fierce array of sharp teeth, make these reptiles efficient fish predators. Able to power their way underwater with a huge muscular tail and webbed feet, they turn their head from side to side to snatch a fish.

Gharials get their name from the ghara, a bulbous growth on the end of mature male snouts that produces a curious buzzing sound which attracts females. When ready to lay their eggs a female climbs out of water onto sandy banks to excavate her nest hole. But the collection of river sand for building has reduced gharial nesting sites.

The crocodilian body has remained unchanged for eons, proof that the design and function have been an evolutionary success.

An ancient lineage

Many of the world's rarest animals are now confined to remote islands where they are not hunted and few, if any, predators exist. The tuatara is an ancient lizard-like reptile found in New Zealand. Once present on the two main islands, hunting of adults, habitat loss and predation of their eggs by the Polynesian rat (*Rattus exulans*), introduced by Maori around 800AD, probably wiped them out by the 1700's, on all but offshore islands. Today, tuatara (the Maori name used both in the singular and the plural) occur on several rather inaccessible rat-free islands off the north-east coast of the North Island and in the Cook Strait.

Along with the Polynesian rat, known locally as *kiore*, two more species of *Rattus* were brought to New Zealand by explorers and sailors; Norway rats (*R. norvegicus*) in the eighteenth century followed by the ship rat (*R. rattus*) in the nineteenth century. These species contributed to the decline of the tuatara together with some of the native flightless birds.

Opposite: A Cook Strait tuatara (*Sphenodon* spp.) basks by day on Takapourewa (Stephens Island) in the Cook Strait, separating the North and South Islands of New Zealand.

Map of New Zealand
with locations of fossilized tuatara and living animals.

- Northern tuatara
- Cook Strait tuatara
- Brothers Island tuatara
- Locations of tuatara fossils

Originally thought to be a lizard, the tuatara was later placed in an ancient group of reptiles known as Rhynchocephalians (beak-heads) or Sphenodontians, which appeared in the Mesozoic some 220 mya alongside early dinosaurs. The tuatara is the sole survivor of this group, fossil evidence shows this lineage once existed in Europe, Africa, Madagascar and South America but died out some 100 mya. Before the ancient super continent Gondwana began to fragment, tuatara ancestors became isolated on the part that separated to become New Zealand.

Often referred to as a living fossil, the tuatara is not identical to its early relatives even though it does possess some characteristics quite distinct from modern lizards. One of these is a parietal or 'third' eye found under the skin on the top of the head with both a lens and a retina and connected by nerves to the brain; it is thought to be light sensitive and to act as a light meter. Tuatara have a much lower temperature tolerance than most reptiles, with a body temperature range of only 7-17°C (45-63°F), although it can rise briefly when they bask by day. So it is not surprising they live life at a very slow metabolic rate and are most active during warm, wet weather. This slow pace of life enables them to survive if food is spasmodic.

Above: The 2.6 square kilometre (one square mile) Takapourewa that rises from the sea with sheer cliffs, is home to 90 percent of the world's population of tuatara.

Right: A male Cook Strait tuatara scales a tree at night on Takapourewa. The leisurely metabolic rate of these reptiles enables them to live for up to a century or more.

Below: Nocturnal reptiles, including the tuatara, have vertical slit pupils, which dilate by night to aid nocturnal vision when hunting.

Above: The spiny crest starts behind the head and runs down the back of a tuatara, which means 'old spiny back' in the Maori language.

Right: Leaf litter covers the floor inside the wind-pruned forest on Takapourewa. After the lighthouse was built and a farm established in 1894, nearly 80 percent of the forest was destroyed and replaced by pasture. When the Department of Conservation (DOC) took over control of the island in 1989, reforestation was a major objective.

Opposite: A Cook Strait tuatara emerges from the burrow it shares with fairy prions (*Pachyptila turtur*) on Takapourewa.

Until quite recently all tuatara were treated as a single species – *Sphenodon punctatus*. Now this has been split into two subspecies: the northern tuatara (*S. p. punctatus*) which lives on islands off the north-east coast of New Zealand; and the Cook Strait tuatara not yet given a subspecific name. The much rarer and smaller Brother's Island tuatara confined to North Brother Island in the Cook Strait, was described as a distinct species in 1877, but was not allocated its own specific name (*S. guntheri*) until over a century later. With only some 400 individuals of this species remaining, it was decided to introduce some to nearby islands: in 1995, 68 Brother's Island tuatara were transferred to Titi Island in the Cook Strait and later another 54 animals were introduced to Matui Island.

Having lived in New Zealand as a child, I had longed to see a wild tuatara. It took me a year to get the necessary permit to visit Stephens Island late in 1977. The only way I could land above the sheer cliffs rising up to 305 metres (1,000 feet) was to crawl into a wooden crate and be winched up off the boat deck. After landing, I walked up to meet the lighthouse keeper and his family who shared the island with 30,000 tuatara!

Above from left to right: Tuatara prey includes: female tree weta (*Hemideina thoracica*) feeds at night on tree trunk; a male cave weta, with extremely long antennae; and fairy prion chicks which resemble outsized powder puffs, are eaten in the summer when insects are scarce. Tuatara teeth wear down with age and are not replaced, so older animals eat soft prey such as earthworms, larvae and slugs.

Tuatara are burrowing reptiles that usually live in seabird burrows made by petrels, prions and shearwaters but they are able to dig their own. Droppings from these birds help to fertilise the burrow soil, creating perfect conditions for insects, spiders and earthworms to flourish and

provide food for the tuatara for much of the year. On Takapourewa, tuatara share the burrows of fairy prions within a stunted forest created by constant pruning from salt-laden winds. The prions come ashore to breed during the austral summer from October to January. In this season the favoured food of the tuatara – curious large-headed insects known as wetas – are scarce so they feed on prion eggs and chicks – the latter are dragged from their burrow before being eaten.

Liquids are gained solely from food, as tuatara drink no water. A ferocious bite with well-developed jaw muscles, plus unique dentition whereby a single row of teeth in the lower jaw fits into a groove between two rows of upper teeth, allows the tuatara to easily devour insect chitin or bony prey.

Opposite: Tuatara are most active at night when they crawl up tree trunks in search of wetas.

Right: Head of Cook Strait tuatara shows the spiny crest and the single row of small teeth fused to the lower jaw.

Above: Tuatara are mentioned in several Maori legends, now they are regarded as a taonga (treasure). This Maori carving depicts two tuatara between the legs of a man.

Right: A tuatara pauses outside its burrow, showing shed tail which will regrow.

Left: When tuatara were featured on four New Zealand stamps in 1991, it helped to raise awareness of this special reptile.

Tuatara are nocturnal, but they may emerge to bask outside the burrow entrance by day. They have a large head and a long tail, with a crest of white spines – most obvious in males – that runs along the back, neck and head. It takes 9-13 years before tuatara breed, when males compete for a mate using terrestrial displays with their spiny crests erect. Mating takes place from January to March and the female lays 8-15 eggs from October to December, which take up to 15 months to develop – the longest incubation period of any reptile. Temperature affects the sex ratio, with warm soil giving rise to males and cooler soils to females. To avoid predation by adults young hatchlings hide under logs and stones, living a diurnal life.

Females breed once every two to five years, however the males are able to breed more frequently and this leads to aggressive behaviour between males owing to the shortage of receptive females.

Even though the tuatara has changed little in appearance over millions of years, the latest research has found when the DNA of modern tuatara is compared with 8000-year-old tuatara bones, the reptile is evolving faster than any other animal so far studied.

A great deal of work has been done to help conserve this unique reptile with an ancient lineage. On islands with rats still present and only a few tuatara remaining, the reptiles were caught and kept in captivity until all the rats had been eradicated. Eggs were collected for captive rearing so they could be reintroduced. Thanks to reintroductions, tuatara now occur on over 30 offshore islands.

For the first time in two centuries, a tuatara nest was found in 2008 on the New Zealand mainland at Karori Wildlife Sanctuary – only minutes away from the capital, Wellington. In 2005, 70 tuatara were donated to the sanctuary from Takapourewa by their *kaitiaki* (guardians) and a further 130 animals released in 2007.

Mobile homes

The ancestors of turtles and tortoises date back to the Triassic – some 220 mya. They roamed the Earth with the earliest dinosaurs, sharing characteristics of living turtles and tortoises, namely an upper carapace or shell over the back and a lower plastron on the underside forming a protective mobile home.

As turtles have evolved over millions of years, they have moved in and out of oceans, with modifications to their limbs, head and body size leading to gigantic turtles developing during the Cretaceous. One of the largest known was *Archeon*, which reached 4.6 metres (15 feet) long and had a head one metre (three feet) long. Modern sea turtles appeared about 110 mya, with a space in the skull for the salt glands used for excreting excessive salt.

The successive stages of turtle evolution are constantly being updated as new fossils come to light. In the case of aquatic turtles, the 2004 discovery of *Eileanchelys waldmani* could be a vital link bridging the gap between early terrestrial and modern aquatic turtles. Found on the Isle of Skye in Scotland, it dates back to the middle Jurassic (164 mya), when it lived in a warmer climate with other aquatic vertebrates, including sharks and salamanders.

Above: A hawksbill turtle (*Eretmochelys imbricata*) swims in shallow water showing enlarged front flippers.

Opposite: A giant tortoise pauses on the rim of Alcedo Crater, Isabela, Galápagos.

Above: One of many turtle skeletons strewn on the floor of Turtle Tomb within the coral island of Sipadan off north-east Borneo. The cavern system, which extends back some 40 metres (131 feet) was discovered by Jacques Cousteau. After swimming inside to escape predation these reptiles presumably drowned when they failed to find an exit.
Photo by Jeff Collett/Natural Visions

Right: Underside of angulate tortoise (*Chersina angulata*) shell showing colour of the plastron and the growth lines, Cape Peninsula National Park, South Africa.

A few years later an even more primitive turtle fossil (220 mya), unearthed in southern China, shed light on how turtle shells may have evolved. *Odontochelys semitestacea* had an incomplete carapace but a fully formed plastron, suggesting the latter formed first as protection against attack by aquatic predators from below. Unlike modern turtles that have a beak, *O. semitestacea* had teeth.

The carapace of tortoises and turtles is made from vertebrae and other bones fused together overlaid with scutes or large scales; the whole structure is strengthened by ribs beneath. There are many variations within this basic design, including reduced scutes. These reptiles tend to be either brown or have yellow and black markings. Some of the smaller tortoises have contrasting coloured rays or rings on the scutes above; while others together with turtles have beautiful patterns on the plastron below.

The age of many bony-shelled tortoises and turtles can be gauged by counting the growth lines on the scutes covering the plastron. Young turtles are easier to age than old ones when the spaces between the growth lines become barely discernible.

Above: The high-domed leopard tortoise (*Geochelone pardalis*), found in African savanna from Sudan down to the southern Cape, has an attractive shell.

Left: The striking shell pattern of the Indian star tortoise (*Geochelone elegans*) makes it much sought after in the exotic pet trade.

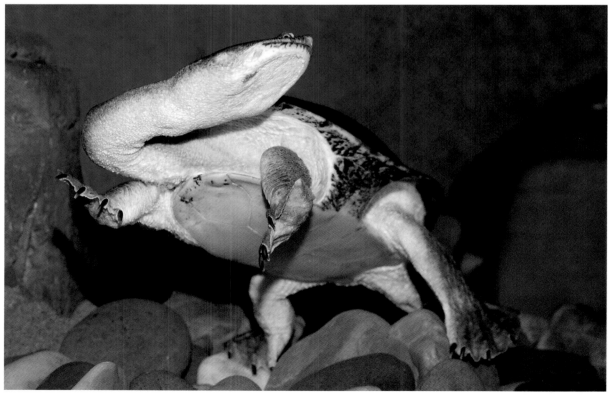

Most tortoises and turtles are able to withdraw their heads, if not their tails and limbs into the shell, closing the front opening with their forelimbs. Notable exceptions are sea turtles; and the big-headed turtle (*Platysternon megacephalum*), with a massive head that remains outside the shell, but is protected by bony armour. Turtles and tortoises are classified into two major groups based on the way they withdraw their head into the shell. Most are the so-called hidden-necked turtles, which bend their neck in a vertical S-shaped curve; while the side-necked turtles retract their heads by bending the neck to one side. Some tortoises have a hinged plastron which allows them to tuck their head in and close the front of their shell when danger threatens.

Above: Underside of Malayan box turtle (*Cuora amboinensis*) showing plastron hinged in the centre, which seals in the entire animal after it withdraws inside the protective shell, Sarawak.

Opposite top: A popular aquarium pet, the yellow-bellied slider (*Trachemys scripta scripta*) withdraws its head straight back into the shell, creating rolls of excess skin.

Opposite: To tuck its head into the shell margin, a sandstone longneck turtle (*Chelodina burrungandjii*) has to bend its neck in a serpentine fashion. These turtles live in streams and billabongs on the Arnhem Land plateau in the Northern Territory (NT), Australia.

Giant tortoises with their large heavy shells adopt a lumbering gait as they move around on land to graze; whereas several aquatic turtles have lightweight shells, with a streamlined profile well suited to chase their aquatic prey. By no means all tortoises and turtles have a complete hard boxed armour; aquatic softshell turtles have a reduced shell covered by a leathery skin as an adaptation for burrowing into soft bottoms. Here they ambush unsuspecting invertebrate prey and can remain on the bottom whilst extending their long neck up to the surface, like a snorkel, to breathe

The matamata turtle (*Chelus fimbriatus*) also uses an ambush technique. The head and neck is covered with fleshy projections that sway in the current just like weeds or algae and are sensitive to water movements made by fish. The way a matamata feeds is unique. It extends the head towards the prey, opens the mouth and expands the throat very suddenly, thereby creating a suction action that draws in water with the prey like a vacuum cleaner. After the mouth is closed the water is slowly ejected before the fish is swallowed whole.

Another devious means of catching prey is adopted by the alligator snapping turtle (*Macroclemys temminckii*), which has a huge head with powerful jaws. Inside the mouth a small pink worm-like lure is wriggled to attract fish by day. This turtle also actively hunts crayfish, frogs and even other turtles as well as being a scavenger.

Top: The pig-nosed turtle (*Carettochelys insculpta*) is regarded as a living fossil, being the sole living member of a single genus within the family Carettochelyidae. Found in the NT, Australia and in New Guinea, it has a shell covered with a soft skin and a pig-like proboscis.

Above middle: The head and neck of a matamata turtle resemble dead leaves in which it burrows, lying in wait for its prey in the Orinoco and Amazon river basins in the north of South America.

Above: Primitive looking baby alligator snapping turtles, with bloodworms as food, for sale in a Hong Kong aquarists' shop. Few people appreciate these diminutive babies will eventually grow into the largest freshwater turtle with a ferocious bite.

48

Above: A Galápagos giant tortoise, which can weigh up to 250 kilos (551 pounds), feeds on grassy patch on the floor of Alcedo Crater on Isabela.

Satellite tracking has revealed the long distance movements of sea turtles from feeding grounds to their nesting beaches. On some beaches, olive ridley turtles (*Lepidochelys olivacea*) come ashore *en masse* to dig their nests and lay their eggs – a phenomenon known in Spanish as an *arribada*. The policy of producing vast numbers of offspring at the same time overwhelms predators, but also gives the impression this turtle is very abundant. Yet, over-

Above: A hawksbill turtle surfaces to breathe whilst swimming.

Left: A mass nesting or *arribada* of female olive ridley turtles coming and going on Playa Ostional on the Pacific coast of Costa Rica.
Photo by Doug Perrine/SeaPics.com

eat an array of marine invertebrates such as crabs, bivalves, barnacles and sea squirts as well as seaweeds, fish and fish eggs. These turtles are attracted to drifting logs and other floating objects that become encrusted with barnacles and other marine organisms.

Adult hawksbill turtles that frequent tropical reefs and lagoons, have found a unique way to avoid competition for food by feeding on sponges. One of the smallest sea turtles, young hawksbills feed on invertebrates but gradually their gut adapts to cope with the sharp glass-like spicules found within their new sponge diet. For centuries, the hawksbill has been hunted for its beautiful patterned amber-coloured shell with coloured rays. The exquisite shell – known misleadingly as tortoiseshell – has been prized for jewellery, ornamental combs and fans, as well as furniture inlay. Even though trading in tortoiseshell was banned, hawksbills remain critically endangered.

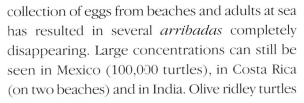

collection of eggs from beaches and adults at sea has resulted in several *arribadas* completely disappearing. Large concentrations can still be seen in Mexico (100,000 turtles), in Costa Rica (on two beaches) and in India. Olive ridley turtles

Above: A green turtle on a coral reef off Sipadan Island in Malaysia.
Photo by Anne Norris/Natural Visions

Right: Safety in numbers: synchronous hatching of baby green turtles foils predators as they head to the sea at dawn, Sarawak.
Photo by Slim Sreedharan/Natural Visions

It is hard to believe that green turtles (*Chelonia mydas*) were once so abundant in the Caribbean Sea, grazing on extensive underwater sea grass meadows, that ships could not avoid making contact with them. Indeed, in 1503, when Columbus discovered the Cayman Islands, he named them Las Tortugas. Their name is derived not from their shell colour, but the greenish fat and cartilage which was used for making turtle soup.

After courtship and mating, female turtles and tortoises lay their shelled eggs either in nests dug from the ground or beneath decaying plants. In the case of sea turtles, the females move out of the sea onto a sandy beach, usually at night, to excavate their nest hole above the tideline. Having laid up to 100 spherical eggs, a green turtle uses her flippers to cover the nest before returning to the sea. Sometimes her eggs are unearthed and eaten by raccoons, coyotes and coatis. Like crocodilians, temperature controls the sex of tortoises and turtles. At low

Above: Lacking teeth, turtles such as this green turtle, rely instead on their horny beak made of keratin to rasp their food.
Photo by Anne Norris / Natural Visions

temperature 28°C (82°F) males develop and females at 31°C (88°F) with a mixture in between. When the hatchling turtles emerge they have to fend for themselves scampering towards the ocean in an attempt to avoid aerial predation by birds. Even once they reach the sea they are eaten by fish and saltwater crocodiles.

Left: The endangered ploughshare tortoise (*Geochelone yniphora*) has a large domed shell with the plastron drawn out into a plough-like projection. It is being bred in captivity at the Ampijoroa scientific station in Madagascar.

Below: As a female leatherback turtle lays eggs, she attracts a crowd on a Malaysian beach at night.
Photo by Slim Sreedharan/Natural Visions

The largest of the seven sea turtles, the leatherback turtle (*Demochelys coriacea*), exists on a diet of jellyfish and other soft-bodied invertebrates. Instead of having bony plates covering the carapace, it has seven ridges, and a flexible shell covered with a leathery skin. The front flippers are huge. Unlike other reptiles, leatherbacks can migrate into cold sea water and dive to below 1,000 metres (3,280 feet) in search of their prey. They are able to do this by maintaining a body temperature several degrees higher than the sea water.

Tortoises occur in tropical and subtropical regions but are absent from Australia. They range in size from the diminutive nine centimetres (3.5 inches) long speckled Cape tortoise (*Homopus signatus*), to the more than 120 centimetres (47 inches) long Galápagos giant tortoises

Top: During the rainy season, giant tortoises that live in Alcedo Crater on Isabela, wallow overnight in temporary pools. They emerge in the morning to graze, lumbering over the floor and even climbing up to the crater rim.

Above: Mud glorious mud! A Galápagos giant tortoise treats itself to a mud wallow in a temporary pool, in Alcedo Crater. These tortoises can live for well over a century.

Opposite: Giant tortoises groan as they mate inside Alcedo Crater. The males, like other male hard shelled tortoises, have a concave plastron so they can mount the domed shell of the female to mate with her.

When Charles Darwin visited the Galápagos, he learnt that the shell shape of giant tortoises varied from island to island. Those that graze on low vegetation have typical domed shells, whereas the ones which live on arid islands and browse on cacti, have a narrow saddle-backed shell so the head and neck can stretch up to reach the cacti pads. Nonetheless, the giant tortoises are thought to belong to a single species – *Geochelone elephantopus*, with distinct races or subspecies on different islands.

Once widespread throughout the archipelago, their numbers declined when buccaneers landed in the 1600s to repair their boats and stocked up with live tortoises, kept for months as a ready source of fresh meat. Over several centuries some 100,000 giant tortoises may have been hunted, with the result that three of the 14 races are now extinct and a fourth race has just a single, male survivor. Coastal tortoises were easiest to collect so that the largest populations are now found in the highland regions.

Giant tortoises probably reached the Galápagos either floating out to sea on currents or on small vegetated islands washed down rivers from the Ecuador mainland – even today vast quantities of vegetation can be seen floating down the flooded Guayas River in Guayaquil.

The evolution of outsized animals – known as gigantism – occurred in many islands where there were no predators and the animals did not have to compete for food. Giant tortoises also occur in the Seychelles, notably the Aldabra giant tortoise (*Dipsochelys dussumieri* or *Geochelone gigantea*) which lives on Aldabra atoll. The Seychelles giant tortoise (*D. hololissa*) and Arnold's giant tortoise (*D. arnoldi*) are so rare, they exist only as a handful of individuals.

Dragons and monitors

The most powerful lizards are the carnivorous dragons and monitors belonging to the genus *Varanus*, many of which have a long neck with loose folds of skin and a pointed head. Varanids have a widespread distribution in a broad band sweeping across Africa, the Middle East and much of Asia to Australia. Most live a terrestrial existence, walking or running with a swinging gait; produced by the foreleg on one side and the hind leg on the other advancing at the same time, so that the head, body and tail undulate from side to side. They are the only lizards with a long forked tongue, which is repeatedly extended to 'taste' the surroundings. When the tip of the tongue is inserted into the Jacobson's organ – in the roof of the mouth – it reads the chemical information picked up from the immediate environment and determines whether it relates to food, threats or a mate, so the monitor can then react in an appropriate way.

Opposite: Sand goanna or Gould's monitor (*Varanus gouldii*) races up a red sand dune at first light, near Alice Springs, Australia.

Right: A perentie extends its long forked tongue to 'taste' the surroundings, NT, Australia.

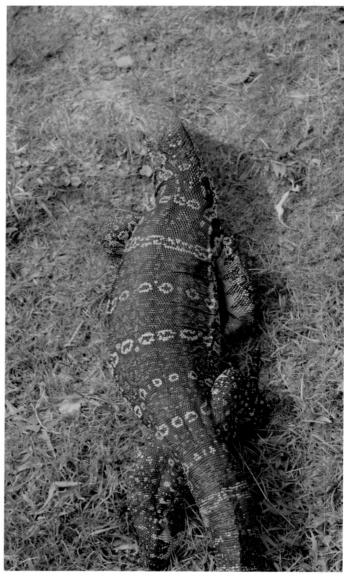

Above: Unusually for monitors, the Salvador's or crocodile monitor (*Varanus salvadorii*) has a blunt nosed head. It is an agile climber and the natives of Papua New Guinea use the smooth skin to make Kundu drums.

Right: The patterned body of an Asiatic water monitor (*Varanus salvator*) shows more clearly after it has emerged from water in Yunnan, China.

Some monitors climb trees with great agility, using their strong claws to grip the trunk, while a few are able to stand up on their hind legs to get an elevated view or to box a rival. Many are also good swimmers, flattening their limbs alongside the body which is moved by sinuous movements of the tail.

The heaviest and most fearsome of all is the Komodo dragon (*Varanus komodoensis*) which can reach two to three metres (6.5–10 feet) in length. It occurs on several islands within Komodo National Park, now a World Heritage Site, in Indonesia.

But Komodo dragons are small fry compared to an extinct giant ripper lizard known as *Varanus priscus* (formerly *Megalania prisca*) that was thought to reach some five metres (16 feet) long, but recent examination of bones has downsized it to an average 3.5 metres (11.5 feet) long. Living in Australia during the Pleistocene until some 50,000–20,000 years ago, it is quite possible that early Aboriginal settlers came across them.

Above: A Nile monitor (*Varanus niloticus*) climbs up a tree to feed on bait at Samburu, Kenya.

Left: An Asiatic water monitor swims with the legs pressed against its body to provide a more streamlined shape in Yunnan, China.

Komodo dragons eat live prey (from small rodents to water buffalo) as well as carrion. Once this dragon bites, its prey is doomed; for septic bacteria living on remnants of flesh amongst the teeth get into the saliva so that even large animals die a few days later from septicaemia. Providing a dragon is downwind from the corpse, it can be detected up to four kilometres (2.5 miles) away as the dragon walks swinging the head from side to side flicking out its tongue. Komodo dragons mostly lead a solitary existence, although they will converge on a carcass to feed, with the largest animals feeding first.

The Komodo dragon shares with other varanids a hinged lower jaw which opens wide to allow them to swallow large prey. In fact, it can eat up to 80 percent of its body weight in a single meal. If it then needs to make a speedy get away it reduces the excess weight by vomiting the stomach contents.

Above: A Komodo dragon with carcass on Komodo Island.
Photo by Soames Summerhays / Natural Visions

All dragons and monitors lay eggs in burrows or hollow trees and even termite mounds. The Komodo dragon lays some 20 eggs, guarding them for over half a year. After hatching, the young dragons dash up trees to escape predation by cannibalistic adults. They will even roll in faeces to avoid predation.

Captive female Komodo dragons, such as Flora at Chester Zoo, have produced eggs, which hatched without being fertilised by sperm – a virgin or parthenogenetic birth. Komodo dragons have the ZW chromosomal sex-determination system and, unlike humans, females carry one W and one Z chromosome. Unfertilised eggs that receive a Z chromosome become ZZ (male); those that receive a W chromosome become WW and fail to develop.

Above: Flora, a female Komodo dragon at Chester Zoo, has twice laid eggs that gave rise to parthenogenetic offspring.

Above right and below left: A male Komodo dragon hatched at Chester Zoo from an egg laid by Flora, without physical contact with a male dragon. Long, sharp claws are used to climb and dig burrows in the wild. The tongue is flicked out to 'taste' the surroundings.

Below: A captive Komodo dragon produces poisonous saliva that dribbles from the jaws and has bad breath.

Above: Even when an Asiatic water monitor swims, the tongue is flicked out periodically, Yunnan, China.

Right: The world's longest lizard, the crocodile monitor, can reach more than three metres (10 feet) in length. Serrated teeth scissor across each other to rip and tear flesh – like *T. rex*!

Opposite: A Bengal monitor (*Varanus bengalensis*) seizes a crab on a sandy shore, Sri Lanka.

Photo by Doug McCutcheon/Natural Visions

The water monitor is the most widespread Asian species; it has a more pointed snout than the Komodo dragon and can grow up to three metres (9.8 feet) long, although most are half this length. Being able to move equally well on land or water, it has a varied diet including terrestrial prey (birds, snakes and diminutive mouse deer), aquatic life (crabs and fish), as well as carrion. These monitors are known to congregate on turtle nesting beaches to eat the eggs and newly hatched turtles. Water monitors may fall prey to large snakes, but if one follows it up a tree overlooking water, the monitor can escape by leaping into the water.

The northernmost of all varanid lizards and one of the most widespread, is the desert monitor (*Varanus griseus*), reaching 46°N up to the Caspian and Aral seas. It occurs right across northern Africa (except for the Atlas Mountains), the Arabian Peninsula and into western Asia. Principally a desert species, this monitor also lives in coastal plains wherever there is sandy soil in which it can burrow and feed on turtle eggs. However, it avoids coastal strips which are splashed with salt spray.

The desert monitor has a variable colour with darker bars across the back and tail, which makes up half of the one metre (3.3 feet) long body. Young lizards have black bands on a vivid orange body. Three distinct subspecies are recognised, with the largest living furthest north and the smallest in the south.

Desert monitors are active from March/April to October/November; thereafter they hibernate underground as the temperature drops. The degree of activity of these diurnal reptiles is directly related to the outside temperature, with 35-38°C (95-100°F) being the optimum. About an hour before sunset they cease being active.

Right: A desert monitor in a sea of sand in the Sahara Desert has nostrils close to its eyes, so it breathes more easily when burrowing into the sand.
Photo by Jason Venus/Natural Visions

Below: The striped body of a desert monitor exposes the forked tongue with a dark tip in the Western Negev Desert, Israel.
Photo by Guy Haimovitch

Monitors, in general, are opportunist predators, feeding mainly on vertebrates by digging rodents from burrows and using their powerful bite to suffocate them. Lizards, snakes and hedgehogs are also taken and shaken vigorously from side to side to kill them. As well as feasting on the eggs and chicks of ground-nesting birds, desert monitors will climb trees to raid nests. They are known to scavenge on roadkills along the coast of Israel. Monitors in Pakistan, on the other hand, feed largely on insects. Desert monitors obtain most of their water via food, but when water is plentiful, they can store up to 15 percent of their weight in body tissues.

Another wide ranging species is the two metres (six feet) long Nile monitor which lives throughout much of Africa, apart from desert regions. Like snakes, it swallows its prey – which includes reptiles, crabs, fish and giant land snails – whole. Two Nile monitors will co-operate when foraging on crocodile eggs, after one lures the female from her nest, the other moves in to unearth the eggs and feeds on them shortly joined by the other partner in crime. Monitors can adopt a threatening posture by opening the mouth, inflating their neck and hissing.

Opposite: The dark forked tongue of a Nile monitor.

Above: To gain a higher vantage point a perentie extends its long neck.

Below: An inquisitive Nile monitor emerges from the Chobe River in Botswana.

Below left: Detail of perentie skin: an Australian legend tells how the perentie got its pattern – a bucket of paint was thrown on the lizard's back!

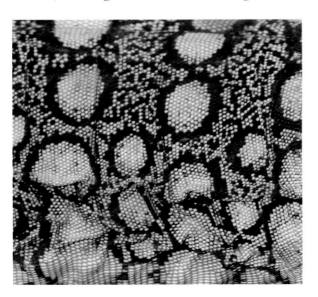

Above: At first light, a Gould's monitor raises its belly off the red sand near Alice Springs in Australia.

Right: When a perentie gallops up a steep sand dune each leg moves in sequence so that the two on each side of the body are either splayed out or overlapping.

Opposite: A fresh perentie track left in sand before the wind obliterated it.

Australia has 20 different kinds of monitor lizards (known locally as goannas); the largest being the perentie or gigantic lace lizard which can reach over two metres (six feet) in length. Perenties are top predators, feeding on small mammals – including the introduced European rabbit (*Oryctolagus cuniculus*) – birds, insects, reptiles (they are known to be cannibalistic); while large adults will even go for small kangaroos. These monitors, which were the favourite food of desert Aboriginals, can stand up on their hind legs and tail – a practice known as 'tripoding' – to gain a better view around them, and can run fast over short distances on their hind legs.

The Gould's monitor or sand goanna is widespread in north and east Australia. A favourite food is crocodile eggs, which helps to keep the crocs in check but these monitors also feed on small agamid lizards, mice, snakes and large insects. It is not uncommon to see these monitors turn over rocks in search of prey. In recent years, cane toads (*Bufo marinus*) have been wiping out goannas in the north.

Although widespread and numerous, monitors generally are at risk as many species are hunted for their meat, medicinal properties and decorative skins; while live specimens are collected for the growing pet trade.

Notable lizards

This chapter touches on the diverse range of lizards, excluding dragons and monitors already covered. Essentially lizards have four limbs, external ears and a protective covering of scales. In terms of sheer number of species, lizards are a highly successful reptilian group: living in tropical, subtropical and temperate parts of both the Old and New Worlds. The most familiar, are those seen basking in the sun; nocturnal species include the many geckos that emerge at night and scurry across walls in houses.

Crocodile skinks are one of only a few lizards – other than geckos – that can vocalise when in distress. Skinks usually have smooth scales but the red-eyed crocodile skink (*Tribolonotus gracilis*) has very spiky scales around the triangular head and along the back and sides with the result that it resembles a miniature crocodile.

Opposite: Chameleons intent on fighting in Madagascar rely on their prehensile tails as an anchorage point.

Below: Found in tropical forests in New Guinea, the red-eyed crocodile skink has a triangular head with an orange eye ring and spiny crocodile-like scales on the body.

The marine iguana is the world's sole marine lizard, the blunt snout allows it to rasp algae growing on rocks in the intertidal zone and also on shallow underwater reefs. The home of the marine iguana straddles the equator, but apart from El Niño years, the Galápagos Islands are washed by the cold water Humboldt Current. After feeding on algae in the sea the iguanas crawl up above the high tide level to bask in colonies on rocks or sand. The smallest marine iguanas with the lowest body mass feed intertidally, as this is a warmer option than plunging into the cold sea.

Above: After a marine iguana enters the sea off the Galápagos, it has to haul out onto rocks to warm up.

Top right: Marine iguanas bask at Punta Espiñosa, Galápagos. Distinct subspecies are found on different islands.

Right: Opuntia cactus fruit provides a source of food and water for land iguanas, which can survive without freshwater for up to a year.

Female marine iguanas haul themselves some 80 metres (262 feet) above the beach to reach sandy ground or volcanic ash deposits, using their sharp clawed feet to aid climbing and to excavate a nesthole. Once there, they may have to compete for a suitable nesting site and can end up head-butting one another. After hatching, the young iguanas have to fend for themselves.

Land iguanas also inhabit the Galápagos; *Conolophus subcristatus* occurs on six islands and has irregular yellow and brown markings on the body. The Barrington or Santa Fe land iguana (*C. pallidus*) has more pronounced spines and a more uniform yellow colouration. When Charles Darwin arrived in the Galápagos in 1835, land iguanas were so numerous; he wrote "…. (on) Santiago Island, we could not for some time find a spot free from their burrows on which to pitch our single tent". This once thriving population has since become completely extinct. Darwin missed seeing the pink iguanas – yet to be given a scientific name – recently discovered on Wolf Volcano on Isabela.

Above: A female marine iguana starts to dig a rest hole on a pebble strewn cliff top on Española, Galápagos.

Below: As a land iguana rests on Las Plazas, in the Galápagos, it evokes the age of the dinosaurs.

Iguanas in general are concentrated in South America and the southern part of North America. A widespread, large, arboreal species is the green or common iguana (*Iguana iguana*), which is not always green. Extending from southern Brazil and Paraguay up to Mexico and the Caribbean Islands, with a feral population in Florida, it has an herbivorous diet and is well adapted for climbing trees and swimming. Green iguanas suffer from being a popular pet and a food source in Central America, where they are nicknamed 'bamboo chicken' or 'chicken of the trees'.

Tegus (*Tupinambis* spp.) are large, tropical South American lizards that are primarily carnivorous. The largest species, the red tegu (*Tupinambis rufescens*) from Argentina is herbivorous. Over a million tegus are slaughtered annually for their attractive glossy bead-like skin which is made into shoes, purses and cowboy boots. They have also become popular in the pet trade.

Right: A male green iguana with a conspicuous dorsal crest, in the process of moulting on Roatan, an island off the north coast of Honduras.

Below right: A basilisk or Jesus Christ lizard (*Basiliscus basiliscus*) – so called for its ability to walk across water – rests in a forest in Manuel Antonio National Park, Costa Rica.

Below: The striking Colombian black and white tegu or common tegu (*Tupinambis teguixin*) is a carnivorous lizard that, like monitor lizards, has sharp teeth and claws.

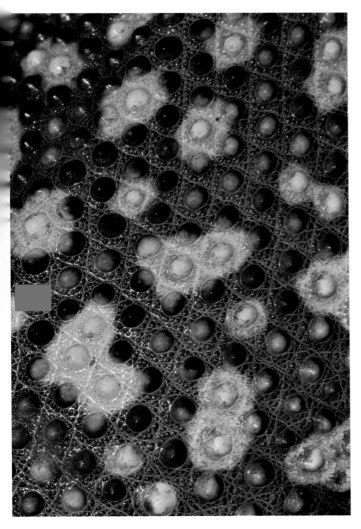

The beaded lizard (*Heloderma horridum*) and the Gila monster (*H. suspectum*) are the only venomous lizards, which is curious since they feed primarily on bird and reptile eggs with the occasional small bird, frog or insect. The *Heloderma* genus dates back to the Miocene when *H. texana* occurred over most of North America and so this genus is regarded as a living fossil. The toxin in the beaded lizard can cause human respiratory failure but the enzymes have been used in producing a drug to combat diabetes.

Living in the south-west deserts of the United States and northern Mexico, Gila monsters can survive dehydration for up to 120 days by reabsorbing water from their urine. When rains come they binge, rehydrating themselves and filling their bladder.

Above: The venomous beaded lizard lives in forests in Guatemala and Mexico, and has a forked tongue.

Above left: The small non-overlapping scales of a beaded lizard resemble polished beads.

Left: Head of a Gila monster shows black and pink body pattern with beaded scales that do not overlap.

Top: A side view of a thorny devil as it pauses near Alice Springs, Australia.

Above: As a thorny devil wicks up water by capillary action via narrow channels between the scales, the body colours become enriched as the water moves up towards the mouth.

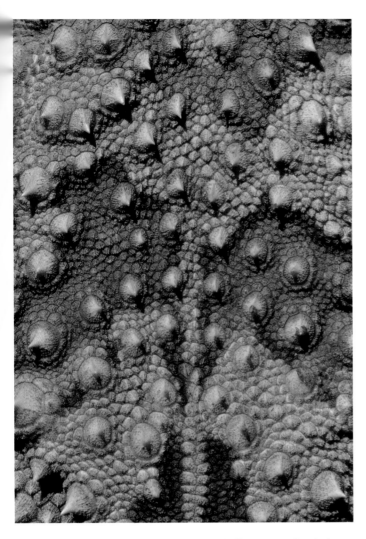

The diversity of lizards in Australian desert far exceeds other desert regions. Scientists are still not sure how so many species can coexist and avoid competition for resources. The variation in feeding habits, the time they are active and chosen microhabitat are all ways to reduce competition. One strategy, which is adopted by the extraordinary thorny devil, is to be a dietary specialist. This species feeds mainly on ants (*Iridomyrmex* spp.); laboriously flicking out its tongue to trap a single ant at a time. Even so, it can still consume several thousand ants in one sitting!

Bearded dragons (*Pogona* spp.), like many desert animals, are typically active in early morning and late in the day, retreating to burrows to avoid the scorching sun. When threatened they puff out their spiny throats and hiss like a cat. Male bearded dragons court a mate by bobbing their head, if a female responds by becoming submissive, the male will grab the back of her head.

Above: The belly pattern of each thorny devil is unique, so it can be used like a fingerprint to identify an animal.

Right: Aggressive posture of a central bearded dragon (*Pogona vitticeps*).

Above: Dark bands on a western blue tongue skink (*Tiliqua occipitalis*) blend in with the shadow patterns of branches and trunks cast on an Australian desert.

Small lizards risk ending up as prey for other reptiles, birds or mammals. Fleeing or bolting down a hole may be one option of escaping, but some lizards have developed cunning survival strategies. Most simply, a cryptic colouration helps them to blend in with their surroundings.

A host of lizards have developed spines on their heads, bodies or tails. The spiny-tailed skink squeezes into rocky crevices in Australia, using its tail as an anchor. The girdle-tailed or armadillo lizard (*Cordylus cataphractus*) turns itself into a spiny covered circular object by grasping the tail in its mouth, making it impossible to swallow. The thorny devil is covered from tip to tail with an impressive array of spines and has several lines of defence. As it moves from bright sunlit patches into the shade, the cryptically coloured body changes colour; if all else fails, the real head is tucked between the forelegs, leaving the spiny false head behind it exposed which makes the lizard difficult to swallow.

The Texas horned lizard (*Phrynosoma cornutum*) also has sharp spines – notably on the head – and a highly original deterrent. By

Above: Two leaf-tailed geckos (*Uroplatus fimbriatus*) blend into a sapling as they rest on Nosy Mangabe, Madagascar.

Above: A rough knob-tailed gecko (*Nephrurus amyae*) opens the mouth to reveal the pink tongue as a threat display.

Below: A centralian blue tongue (*Tiliqua multifasciata*) displays its dark blue tongue as a predator deterrent.

Bottom: The sleepy lizard has an armoured body with a tail that resembles the head and stores fat for winter hibernation.

raising the blood pressure in the head it can squirt out a stream of blood from the corners of the eyes up to 1.2 metres (four feet) at predatory wolves, coyotes and domestic dogs.

Found in Australian deserts, the stump-tailed or sleepy skink (*Tiliqua rugosa*) is a blue-tongued skink. When threatened, this skink has two means of defence. The short, stumpy triangular tail that mimics the head is directed towards the aggressor and when any pressure is put on the tail it fragments and continues to wriggle. While this distracts the predator, the skink is able to get away. If this fails, the skink will suddenly open its mouth towards the threat, displaying the blue tongue and hissing.

A dramatic threat display is shown by the frillneck lizard (*Chlamydosaurus kingii*) – with the mouth agape it unfurls the folded frill around its neck like an umbrella, making it appear much larger than in reality. These lizards run in the desert on all fours but when they accelerate the body flips up and they become bipedal and thus more manoeuvrable. The connection between speed of movement and body stance was discovered by scientists filming lizards on a treadmill.

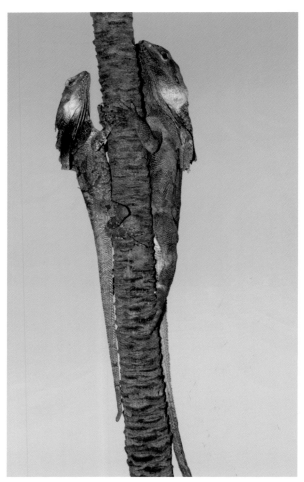

Above: Iberian worm lizard (*Blanus cinereus*) belongs to one of three families of legless lizards. This blind fossorial reptile burrows into the ground in arid locations.

Right: Frilled lizards resting with flattened frills blend in with the palm trunk in the NT, Australia.

Most skinks lack a pronounced neck and have a relatively small tail which can be shed and regenerated. Active arboreal skinks have well developed limbs; whereas those that spend considerable time below ground or under cover have much reduced limbs. There are even legless skinks – notably many species in Africa – which have lost their limbs completely. The Australian skinks are a widespread and diverse lizard group, found from the intertidal zone to mountain tops and include the blue-tongue skinks which give rise to live young.

The sandfish (*Scincus scincus*) is a skink which avoids the scorching desert heat in north Africa, Saudi Arabia, Iraq and Iran by diving into soft sand. It has fine smooth scales covering the body, a wedge-shaped nose and fringed toes which allow it to 'swim' through loose sand. Scientists have discovered that sandfish skin offers less friction than glass or polished steel. High speed X-ray imaging has shown that once beneath the sand, the sandfish holds its limbs against the body which is moved in an S-shaped motion. The bluetail mole skink (*Eumeces egregius egregius*) from Florida is also a 'sand swimmer'.

Endemic to the Namib Desert in Namibia is the shovel-snouted lizard (*Meroles anchietae*), which performs a curious thermal dance to prevent overheating on the hot desert sand. Walking high over the sand, it alternates raising the opposite front and hind legs off the scorching surface.

Above: Sandfish are so-called because they are able to 'swim' through desert sands. Beneath the sand, they are able to sense vibrations of insect prey walking on the sand surface
Photo by Thomas Schmidt/Natural Visions

Left: Shovel-snouted lizard on a sand dune in Namibia.

Anyone who has lived in the tropics or subtropics will be familiar with house geckos that emerge on walls to hunt at night. Climbing geckos are able to walk upside down on ceilings or up slippery glass by a myriad of microscopic adhesive pads on the underside of their feet. Whereas the web-footed gecko (*Palmatogecko rangei*), found in the Namib Desert, has webs between the toes which increase the surface area to prevent it sinking into the sand and also for scooping out burrows.

Geckos have no eyelids, instead the eyes are protected by a transparent covering known as a spectacle. This is kept clean by geckos repeatedly wiping it with their pliable tongue. Nocturnal geckos have large eyes in which the pupil contracts to a narrow slit by day, but when they hunt spiders and insects by night this enlarges to an almost circular shape.

Green day geckos (*Phlesuma* spp.) are found on Madagascar and other Indian Ocean Islands such as the Seychelles and Mauritius, typically spotted crawling up tree trunks to feast on nectar, pollen and fruit as well as insects. They have smaller eyes than the nocturnal species with a round pupil.

Above: Underside of a tokay gecko (*Gekko gecko*) foot shows ridges made up from millions of tiny hairs, called setae, which enable it to walk up walls and even upside down.

Right: New Caledonian crested gecko (*Rhacodactylus ciliatus*) uses its tongue to wash the eye spectacle. Native to southern New Caledonia rainforests; it was thought to be extinct until rediscovered in 1994.

Above: A leaf-tailed gecko rests on a stem and shows its conspicuous tail at Nosy Mangabe, Madagascar.

Below: A colourful day gecko (*Phelsuma madagascariensis grandis*) rests on dry banana leaves in Madagascar.

Top right: A day gecko laps up nectar on an Euphorbia flower in Madagascar.

Above: When a southern spiny-tailed gecko (*Strophurus intermedius*) is attacked it raises the tail and squirts out a sticky amber secretion via spines up to 60 centimetres (23 inches) away. The secretion is pungent and irritating to the eyes and mucous membranes.

85

Above: Underside of a male Yemen chameleon shows the zygodactyl feet in which adjacent digits are fused on each hand and foot, forming opposable grasping pads.

Right: Head on male Yemen chameleon shows independent eye movement.

Opposite: When not in use prehensile tails are neatly coiled, as shown in this striking male Yemen chameleon.

Below: Using high speed X-ray videos it has been found the projectile tongue of a chameleon accelerates five times faster than a fighter jet. Here the sticky tip of a male Meller's chameleon (*Chamaeleo melleri*) grasps a locust before it is withdrawn into the mouth—all in under a second.

The lizards with the greatest appeal have to be the chameleons; not only do they come in an array of attractive colours, but also they are able to rapidly change colour. This is now thought to be a means of communication when they meet a rival, want to attract a mate or as a means of temperature control rather than just to blend in with their surroundings. The stereoscopic eyes can move independently and their ability to capture insect prey with their very long, rapidly extendible tongue is legendary. The five toes on each foot are fused into one group of two and another of three, providing a pincer mechanism for tightly gripping narrow branches. The prehensile tail also acts as an anchor for arboreal chameleons when they move from one branch to another.

Madagascar, the chameleon capital of the world, is home to about half of the 150 chameleon species, ranging in size from the 68 centimetre (2.2 feet) long Parson's chameleon (*Calumma parsonii parsonii*) to the diminutive leaf chameleons (*Brookesia spp.*) that are barely the size of a finger nail and live in the leaf litter.

Chameleons live in tropical and mountain rainforests, savannas and even semi-desert.

Conservation

Above: Reptiles are threatened throughout the world. Turtle and tortoise populations have been depleted by over-collection of adults and eggs for food. Habitat destruction for agriculture and dam building, as well as poaching, has made the Chinese alligator (*Alligator sinensis*) the most threatened crocodilian, with only 150 animals remaining in the wild. However, a successful captive breeding programme (begun in 1979) has produced more than 10,000 hatchlings at the Anhui Breeding and Research Centre.

Left: The introduction of exotic mammals has depleted, if not wiped out, native reptiles — particularly on islands. Cats, rats and mongooses eradicated the Round Island gecko (*Phelsuma guentheri*) from mainland Mauritius and Réunion Island. This gecko is now restricted to Round Island, where tropical cyclones and grazing by goats and rabbits forced it to retreat into crevices within the lava. After removal of these invasive herbivores, the endemic *Latania loddigesii* palm forest is slowly regenerating.

Below: The gharial story is a roller coaster one. After reintroduction, almost half of the world population of wild gharial lived in the Chambal River Sanctuary in North India. In December 2007, 90 gharial corpses were washed up on the banks. Autopsies on these bodies traced the source of the toxin to a highly polluted river a few miles downstream.

Below: Understanding reptile movements and migrations is vital for their conservation, so they are tagged either by attaching a number (gharials, shown here) or by fitting radio collars (tuatara) or radio transmitters (oceanic turtles).

Left: We can see how global warming is threatening polar regions. Perhaps surprisingly, lizards living in tropical forests with a narrow temperature range, will suffer more than lizards found in cooler, more variable climates, if they cannot adapt fast enough to rising temperatures. Even more ominously, the sex ratios of reptiles where the sex is determined by temperature could result in a disastrous imbalance. The Parson's chameleon lives in tropical forests in Madagascar.

Below left: Souvenirs stall with endangered turtles, puffer fish, armadillos and shells outside Pangandaran National Park, Java, Indonesia.
Photo by Giles Angel/Natural Visions

Below: The slaughter of saltwater crocodiles for their skins caused the Australian population to plummet, but it has since recovered after hunting was banned and crocodile farms opened to satisfy the demand for these prized skins.

Photo tips and hints

There are many ways to photograph reptiles, it all depends on their size, their habitat, the time of day (or night) they are active, their behaviour and whether they are resting or moving at speed. Aquatic reptiles, such as the larger crocodiles and alligators that have been known to kill humans, should be taken from the safety of a substantial boat or an overlook.

How reptiles move underwater can be seen when housed in a tank with a large, clear viewing window. Perspex tanks scratch more easily than glass, which will show in a photo when the alligator or crocodile nudges the inside front tank wall. Scratches can, however, be thrown out of focus by waiting for the reptile to move away from the wall and by using a fairly large aperture to give a limited depth of field.

Left: Flash was used to freeze the movement of a sandstone snakeneck turtle in an aquarium

Opposite: For the frame-filling eye of a Parson's chameleon, I opted for a long exposure without flash to avoid an obvious rectangular reflection in the eye.

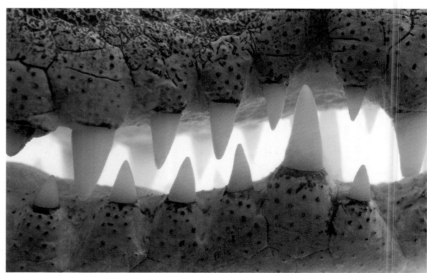

Above: The shadow cast on the sand by the low angled light repeats the shape of the perentie.

Right: Detail of saltwater crocodile jaws shows how the teeth interlock.

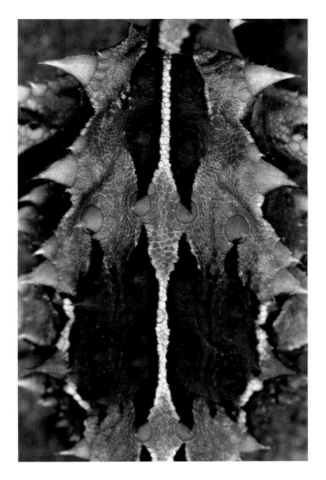

Left: Thorny devil abstract taken from above with a macro lens.

In some places flies can be a real nuisance so that it becomes impossible to concentrate on the photography; when you are so busy extricating flies from the mouth, ears and nostrils, you miss getting an action shot. A fly net will solve this problem but will not prevent frames being peppered with out-of-focus flies.

Terrestrial giant tortoises, dragons and monitors, will look more dramatic if they are taken from a low viewpoint using a wide angle lens, so that part of the animal is seen against the sky. However, care must be taken not to approach a poisonous reptile such as the beaded lizard or the Gila monster too closely.

A glance through this book will show a change of pace as the pages are turned, since it would be very boring to see page after page of a complete reptile on land. Pace can be varied in many ways; by taking some action shots, by featuring a tight crop to highlight dentition or a head feeding. Interesting behaviour also helps to arrest attention, whether it be a gecko's threat display, a monitor flicking out its tongue or a gecko licking its eye. You will, however, need a camera with a very fast reaction time to record the way a chameleon uses its tongue to capture prey or the awesome gaping jaws of a saltwater crocodile underwater.

Information and Acknowledgements

INFORMATION

Notable reptilian collections

Reptile collections constantly evolve – either expanding or contracting – so any listing will soon become out of date. However, a web search for living reptile collections in a specific country will bring up a list.

The following were very helpful and have useful information.

• **Chester Zoo**
Has several monitors and iguanas on view, notably Komodo dragons and is the only place to see tuatara in the UK.
http://www.chester.zoo.org

• **Alice Springs Reptile Centre**
Showcases Northern Territory reptiles in Alice Springs, Australia.
http://esvc000320.wic012tu.server-web.com
Email: rex@reptilecentre.com.au

Internet sites

More information about living reptiles can be found on the following internet sites.

• **ARKive**
A unique collection of thousands of videos, images and fact-files illustrates worldwide species.
Click on Reptiles and select species
http://www.arkive.org

• **CROCODILIANS**
Natural History & Conservation
http://www.crocodilian.com

• **National Geographic**
Provides free maps, photos, videos, articles and features about animals as well as daily news stories.
Click on Animals, then on Reptiles
http://www.nationalgeographic.com

• **Smithsonian National Zoological Park**
Click on Reptiles and Amphibians
http://nationalzoo.si.edu/animals

• **The Spinyback Tuatara Education and Conservation Charitable Trust**
Set up in 2007
http://www.tuataratrust.co.nz

ACKNOWLEDGEMENTS

Many people helped me in the production of this book. My grateful thanks to the New Zealand Department of Scientific and Industrial Research (DSIR) for granting me permission to land on Stephens Island – as Takapourewa was known in 1976. I should especially like to thank Lucy Simpson who did a superb job researching and also proof-

Left: The male Lesser Antilles iguana (*Iguana delicatissima*) has enlarged scales forming a crest along the back and long spikes on the dewlap. When it is reproductively active, the crest turns blue and the jowls flush pink. Habitat destruction, hunting, feral predators as well as hybridisation with the green iguana, have contributed to make this iguana vulnerable.

reading the entire book. Kate Carter also assisted with proof-reading. The following people kindly facilitated photography: most especially Rex Neindorf at Alice Springs Reptile Centre with location photography; Geoff Read at Marwell Zoo; Richard Gibson, curator of Lower Vertebrates and Invertebrates at Chester Zoo; Linda Bridges at Liberty's Raptor and Reptile Centre; the Spectacular Jumping Crocodile cruise *http://www.jumpingcrocodile.com.au* and David Southard at Wild Arena *http://www.wildarena.com* all provided access to reptiles. Ed Pugh assisted in preparing the digital images.

FURTHER READING

• Alderton, David, *Crocodiles and Alligators of the World*, Facts on File, New York, USA, 2004

• Halliday, Tim and Kraig Adler, *The New Encyclopedia of Reptiles and Amphibians*, Oxford University Press, 2004

• Kelly, Lynne, *Crocodile: Evolution's greatest survivor*, Allen & Unwin, London, 2006

• Lutz, Dick, *Tuatara: A Living Fossil*, Dimi Press, Salem, Oregon, USA, 2005

• Spotila, James R., *Sea Turtles: A Complete Guide to Their Biology, Behaviour and Conservation*, The John Hopkins University Press, Baltimore, USA, 2004

• Steel, Rodney, *Living Dragons*, Blandford (Cassell Group), London, 1996

• Webb, Grahame and Manolis, Charlie, *Australian Crocodiles: A Natural History*, Reed New Holland, Sydney, 1998

• Webb, Grahame and Manolis, Charlie, *Australian Freshwater Crocodiles*, G.Webb Pty. Limited, Winnellie, 1988

Other Wildlife Monographs titles published by

EMB Evans Mitchell Books

Wildlife Monographs
Giant Pandas
ISBN: 978-1-901268-13-3

Wildlife Monographs
Monkeys of the Amazon
ISBN: 978-1-901268-10-2

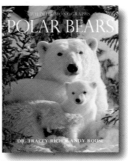

Wildlife Monographs
Polar Bears
ISBN: 978-1-901268-15-7

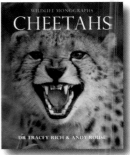

Wildlife Monographs
Cheetahs
ISBN: 978-1-901268-09-6

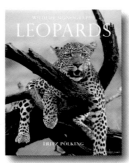

Wildlife Monographs
Loepards
ISBN: 978-1-901268-12-6

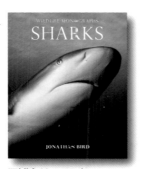

Wildlife Monographs
Sharks
ISBN: 978-1-901268-11-9

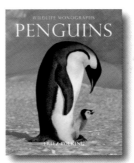

Wildlife Monographs
Penguins
ISBN: 978-1-901268-14-0

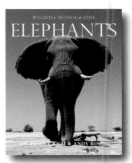

Wildlife Monographs
Elephants
ISBN: 978-1-901268-08-9

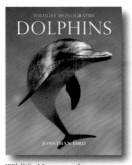

Wildlife Monographs
Dolphins
ISBN: 978-1-901268-17-1

Wildlife Monographs
Wolves
ISBN: 978-1-901268-18-8

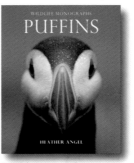

Wildlife Monographs
Puffins
ISBN: 978-1-901268-19-5

Wildlife Monographs
Snow Monkeys
ISBN: 978-1-901268-37-9

Architectural Design
July/August 2008

Protoarchitecture
Analogue and Digital Hybrids

Guest-edited by Bob Sheil

IN THIS ISSUE

Main Section

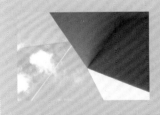

WILEY
wiley.com

Architectural Design

Vol 78 No 4
ISBN 978-047 51947 9

Editorial Offices
John Wiley & Sons
International House
Ealing Broadway Centre
London W5 5DB

T: +44 (0)20 8326 3800

Editor
Helen Castle

Reglar columnists: Valentna Croci, David Littlefield, Jayne Merkel, Vil. McLean, Neil Spiller, Michael Weinstock and Ken Yeang

Freelance Managing Editor
Caroline Ellerby

Production Editor
Elizabeth Gongde

Design and Prepress
Artmedia Press, London

Printed in Italy by Conti T pocclor

Sponsorship/advertising
Faith Pidduck/Wayne Frcst
T: +44 (0)1243 770254
E: fpidduck@wiley.co.uk

All Rights Reserved. No part of this publication may be reproduced, stored in a retrieval system or transmitted in any form or by any means, electronic, mechanical, photocopying, recording, scanning or otherwise, except under the terms of the Copyright, Designs and Patents Act 1988 or under the terms of a licence issued by the Copyright Licensing Agency Ltd, 90 Tottenham Court Road, London W1T 4LP, UK, without the permission in writing of the Publisher.

Front cover: Theo Jansen, Animaris Percipiere, Ijmuiden, The Netherlands, May 2005. © Loek van der Klis

Editorial Board

Will Alsop, Denise Eratton, Mark Burry, André Chaszar, Nigel Coates, Peter Cook, Teddy Cruz, Max Fordham, Massimiliano Fuksas, Edwin Heathcote, Michael Hensel, Anthony Hunt, Charles Jencks, Jan Kaplicky, Bob Maxwell, Jayne Merkel, Michael Rocondi, Leon van Schaik, Neil Spiller Michael Weinstock, Ken Yeang

Subscribe to ᗅᗐ

ᗅᗐ is published bimonthly and is available to purchase on both a subscription basis and as individual volumes at the following prices.

PRICES
Individual copies: £22.99/$45.00
Mailing fees may apply

ANNUAL SUBSCRIPTION RATES
Student: UK£70/US$110 print only
Individual: UK £110/US$ 70 print only
Institutional: UK£180/US$335 print or online
Institutional: UK£198/US$369 combined print and online

Subscription Offices UK
John Wiley & Sons Ltd
Journals Administration Department
1 Oldlands Way, Bognor Regis
West Sussex, PO22 9SA
T: +44 (0)1243 843272
F: +44 (0)1243 843232
E: cs-journals@wiley.co.uk

[ISSN: 0003-8504]

Prices are for six issues and include postage and handling charges. Periodicals postage paid at Jamaica, NY 11431. Air freight and mailing in the USA by Publications Expediting Services Inc, 200 Meacham Avenue, Elmont, NY 11003.
Individual rate subscriptions must be paid by personal cheque or credit card. Individual rate subscriptions may not be resold or used as library copies.

All prices are subject to change without notice.

Postmaster
Send address changes to 3 Publications Expediting Services, 200 Meacham Avenue, Elmont, NY 11003

RIGHTS AND PERMISSIONS
Requests to the Publisher should be addressed to:
Permissions Department
John Wiley & Sons Ltd
The Atrium
Southern Gate
Chichester
West Sussex PO19 8SQ
England

F: +44 (0)1243 770620
E: permreq@wiley.co.uk

CONTENTS

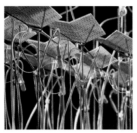

AD+

Editorial

Helen Castle

Lebbeus Woods' summation of Zaha Hadid's approach as 'wringing the extraordinary out of the mundane' is one that could be applied to many of the designers in this issue: whether it is Theo Jansen playing God and creating fantastic beasts out of hundreds of metres of electric cabling; Niall McLaughlin inserting commonplace found objects into screens; or the Koshirakura Landscape Workshop incorporating its readings and reflections on the bucolic Japanese landscape into its constructed projects. For in focusing on prototyping – whether the three-dimensional or the two-dimensional, the handmade or the digital – this issue focuses on the transformative powers of materials aside from the realisation of a built work. It emphasises the importance of investing in and playfully experimenting with generative design, whether that is prototyping as a part of the design process prior to realisation or as with a practice such as Smout Allen where the drawings and models are the project in themselves. No better argument could be put forward for the power of the prototype than Zaha Hadid.

The opportunity to build may have eluded her for a couple of decades of her career, but her time could not have been better spent than on her drawings and paintings – so much being spatially and geometrically explored in two dimensions.

In a sense this issue distils much of what *Architectural Design* has stood for over time as an advocate of the primacy of the generative, literally the importance of design in architecture. It highlights the significance of play, experiment, research and evolution, even allowing space for the random and accidental, for ideas to emerge and develop in a not particularly linear way. It is to Bob Sheil's credit that in guest-editing this issue, which takes in digital and analogue prototypes, that he does not pitch one mode or media against each other. It is very apparent that all the featured architects have distinct preferences and preoccupations. Mark West, for instance, is strident in his use of physical models and hand-drafted drawings but does not hesitate to recognise the usefulness of CAM for calculating structures with complex curves. Mette Ramsgard Thomsen in 'Robotic Membranes' reconciles the automated, electronic world of digital data with the tactile sensuality of textiles. The *modus operandi* is thus one of assimilation, hybridisation and shifts over time. Woods, for example, describes Hadid's changing preoccupations paralleled with her move from hand drawing and painting to the computer. Rather than presenting a picture of media exclusivity or that of binary opposites, Sheil uses the issue to demonstrate how the digital has led to a proliferation of types of work that all invest and rejoice in the prototype. **∆**

sixteen*(makers), Kielder Probes, Kielder Forest, Northumbria, 2007
Prototypes for passively activated and adaptable architecture by sixteen*(makers), Kielder Forest, Northumbria. Acting as architects in residence within the territory of Kielder Forest, sixteen*(makers) have designed and installed a series of experimental assemblies that respond to immediate micro-environmental conditions. The 'Probes', as they are called, are continually monitored by an array of photogrammic instruments that map actual behaviour of the real upon predicted behaviour of the ideal. Seeking a greater understanding of site, the work has developed as a tool for informing and determining architectures that are unique to location (see page 11).

Introduction

Protoarchitecture

Between the Analogue and the Digital

By Bob Sheil

In the post-digital age, how we design has become as important as what we design. Never before have there been so many, or so varied, techniques and methods at our disposal, each with the capacity to leap only previously imagined frontiers. Designing has become a fluid discipline pouring into domains that for centuries have been the sole possession of others, such as mathematicians, neurologists, geneticists, artists and manufacturers. Post-digital designers more often design by manipulation than by determinism, and what is designed has become more curious, intuitive, speculative and experimental. Each of these new techniques vies for dominance in the competitive world of advanced tooling. They battle to outdo one another, predict the unpredictable, promise the unattainable, materialise the immaterial, solve all our problems, and so dazzle the beholder that all previous paths to architectural wonderment pale into the archives.

Our new tools are more malleable than before, so much so that no sooner do they graduate from beta mode than a brighter, fitter, shinier sibling has emerged. As recently as 20 years ago, when I began my architectural education, the methodology of designing buildings had largely remained unchanged in 500 years. Drawings were prepared by hand and evolved from the tentative to the fully costed. Things got built, sometimes in strict accordance with what was drawn, but not always, as records later captured. A few well-known but rare individuals such as Pierre Chareau, the designer of the Maison de Verre in Paris (1932), managed it all without such dogmatic trappings, creating his magnificent *pièce de résistance* in collaboration with Bernard Bijvoet and the craftsman Louis Dalbet, largely through conversation and modelling. Others of the 20th century, such as Anton Gaudi, Richard Buckminster Fuller, Jean Prouvé, Cedric Price and Charles and Ray Eames, also pioneered efforts to rethink the habitual practices of the design process, but the tools to develop it remained largely the same.

Now we are spoilt for choice, and are frantically catching up with the latest definitions on how the design revolution is to unfold. While a diverse and uncertain future is the only plausible outcome, this issue of *AD* is an attempt to cut across rhetoric, prediction, manifesto and obsession regarding what beckons for the near future by taking a temperature reading on the near present. It has been a highly enjoyable task that has taken me from London to New York, Copenhagen, Tokyo, Winnipeg, Ypenburg and back to the warren of cramped rooms that somehow sustain the insatiable Bartlett School of Architecture at UCL. At the outset my ambition for the issue was twofold: to let the diversity and quality of content speak for itself; and to resist editorial temptation to tie it all together or to create an argument. 'Protoarchitecture' is not a recognised word. It is therefore only part real, and that is how I see it – part real, part ideal. It recalls propositions that are prompted by vision rather than convenience. It may be plural or singular, evolutionary or revolutionary, temporary or permanent. It is at once a construct of the physical and the virtual. It does not conform; it is, by definition, an exception. To make things clearer, protoarchitecture is a self-made derivative of 'prototype', a term that conjures up more familiar understandings in design on matters of modelling, experimentation, versioning the basis for other things, and so on.

Ryan Martin (Unit 23/Bartlett), Crypt vault combing instrument, St Olave's Church, City of London, 2007
Installed in the crypt of St Olave's Church, a series of salt-scraping instruments tracked the former frescoed surface. Induced by friction and gravity, they scraped the vaulted ceiling of salts at an imperceptible pace to the eye and deposited a new salt fresco on the floor below.

Rather than imply type as purely an outcome of design, as if they were separate entities, my aim is to suggest how design is bound by the overarching vision of ideas as they transgress from drawing to making.[1] In this regard, my subtitle here, 'Between the Analogue and the Digital', draws upon the significant and growing proportion of work where computation has not colonised the design process. Design is, and should remain, a diverse practice and I am optimistic about its future. In the post-digital age, an increasing proportion of design practices are adopting hybrid modes of experimentation, and even rejuvenating techniques such as hand drawing, model-making, craft or the testing of ideas in actual rather than virtual environments. Techniques that were once consigned to the distant past are being renewed as tools that offer results in a way that digital counterparts cannot. Forthcoming haptic interface technologies and improvements in CAD's simulation of material performance will expand the middle ground. They will become better informed and will run off live data-feeds from actual sites and actual occupation. Buildings will monitor their own performance and provide the template for next generations. However, it is the gap between simulation and actualisation which, as Stephen Gage reminds us (see pages 12–21), makes architecture delightful and surprising. It remains the *raison d'être* of the designer.

If there is anything that is common to each contribution in this issue it is the ubiquitous matter of making ideas manifest as physical constructs. The authors present their work through the considerations that arise when fabrication is taken on as another layer in the creative process. For Mark West of CAST, the developer of the remarkable fabric formwork technique (see pages 50–5), the process of fabrication is quite literally the idea being designed – thinking with matter, as he says. For others, such as Niall McLaughlin (pages 70–9) or Shin Egashira (pages 86–91), what is made is a rich supply of critical reflective material, casting a new light on previous understandings. The inspirational Theo Jansen (pages 22–7) and the meticulous Evan Douglis (pages 62–9) simply let us enjoy the exquisite obsession of their work, and London-based Smout Allen (pages 80–5) allow access to the craftsman-like dexterity and sublime elegance of their drawings, models and unique reading of the landscape. Stephen Gage (pages 12–21) relates more than 60 years of evolutionary research that informs the latest breed of performative artefacts, systems and events emanating from his longstanding unit at the Bartlett, a territory that is echoed in Mette Ramsgard Thomsen's Robotic Membranes (pages 92–7). Lebbeus Woods (pages 28–35) pieces together an extraordinary review on the progression of Zaha Hadid's work from drawings to buildings over a period of 25 years, and contributions from the newly established practices of LIQUID FACTORY (pages 56–61) and Audialsense (pages 98–103) coincidentally deal with the same material for utterly dissimilar purposes.

Having introduced my invited contributors, I now wish to introduce selected protoarchitectural works by recent gradates of the Bartlett's Unit 23, whom I have had the pleasure of tutoring firstly with Graeme Williamson of Block Architecture (2003–06) and now with Emmanuel Vercruysse of Liquid Factory. Together we practise a speculative attitude towards the physical and tactile in architecture. We make to design, and we design to make. Our preoccupations lie

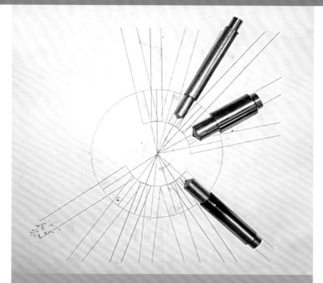

Tim Barwell (Unit 23/Bartlett), Ambient environmental resonator, abandoned observatory, UCL, London, 2007
1:1 template plan of the required positions of the arms into the cast-iron core, overlaid with three bespoke tools (one relating to each size of arm bracket) produced to allow accurate location of milling points.

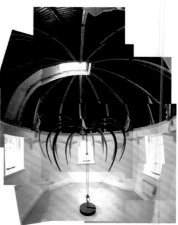

The environmental resonator, installed in the abandoned observatory at UCL, in its extended and contracted positions.

Connected by an array of piano wire to the pumps, the leaves expand and contract 'in tune' with the external ambient temperature. Passers-by can strike the wires and play the musical note of that instant.

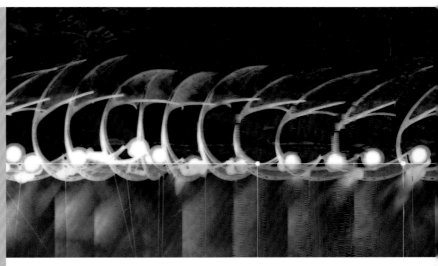

beyond materialisation or mere fabrication, and are formed around the illusive and uncertain world of translating ideas into matter. In this regard, the unit navigates by experimentation, critical intuition, craft and site exploration.

Graduate Tim Barwell, with a background in furniture design and fabrication, has developed considerable skills in making, and chose an abandoned observatory in the grounds of University College London (UCL) for his project. The observatory has remained unused for its original purpose for decades, the night sky long obscured by London's radiance. The opportunity presented itself to imagine what a redundant observatory might observe closer to the ground, and furthermore what might it observe of things we cannot see. The final construct was arrived at through many iterations, after testing humidity, sunlight, user behaviour, material behaviour, air movement and so on. In its ultimate configuration, the ambient resonator stands on the centrepoint of the space. Its 'leaves' are activated by a cluster of orchid wax-filled thermo pumps located on the external crown of the dome. Connected by an array of piano wire to the pumps, the leaves expand and contract 'in tune' with the external ambient temperature. Passers-by can strike the wires and play the musical note of that instant.

Michael Garnett's Flotsam and Jetsam projects are a series of jewellery-like mechanisms designed to record and respond to the micro-environments of London's wasteland. The first was a mechanism that skims along the surface of the Regent's Canal, kept upright by a sub-aqua counterweight, which also acts as a silt-measuring instrument. This was followed by a series of exquisitely crafted monitors located across a number of land and airborne locations in King's Cross, central London's largest construction site. The monitors were inspired by the black redstart, a protected bird species with a mortal attraction to building sites, cement works, refuse tips and decaying structures, all of which can be found in the area. As a protected species, the black redstart can bring a multibillion-dollar construction contract to a halt. All it takes is the sighting of a breeding pair on site. Michael's creations had all the beauty and poise of such a delicate and wonderful creature.

Michael Garnett (Unit 23/Bartlett), Flotsam and Jetsam Mechanism V1, Regents Park, London, 2006
Kept upright by a sub-aqua counterweight, which also acts as a silt-measuring system, the mechanism skims along the water's surface on a seemingly random course, triggering its built-in pinhole camera to record changing patterns of duckweed.

Michael Garnett (Unit 23/Bartlett), Flotsam and Jetsam Mechanism V2, King's Cross, London, 2007
The seismic monitor in the drop position.

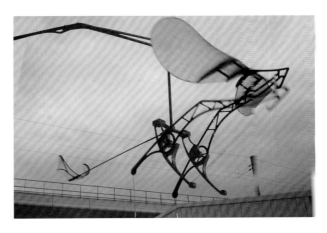

The seismic monitor in the airborne position.

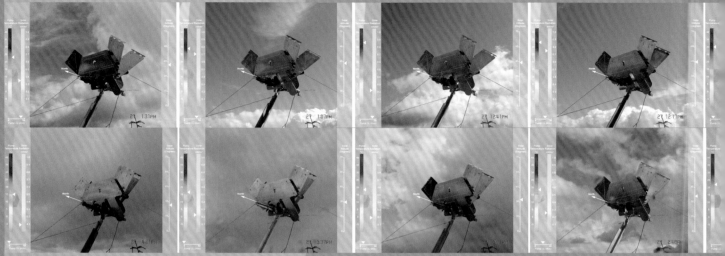

The combing instrument in position.

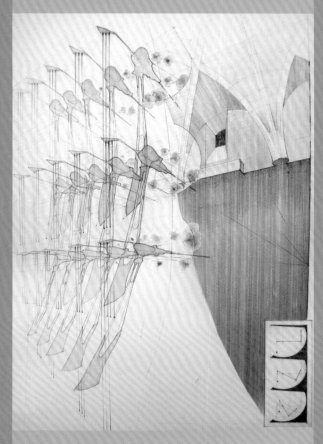

Ryan Martin (Unit 23/Bartlett), Crypt vault combing instrument, St Olave's Church, City of London, 2007
Array study.

sixteen*(makers), Kielder Forest, Northumbria, 2005
A selection of images from a time-lapse survey made on 27 August 2005 on test site B, visualising the physical sensing data collected during an evaluation within its three-dimensional context. The camera viewpoint here is number four of five used to make a 3-D survey of the mechanism using the technique of photogrammetry.

We designed bespoke surveying tools to monitor and respond to local environmental behaviours, and installed them on a test site chosen for its remoteness as well as for its variety, adjacent to an area of dense forestation, an area recently harvested, and an area planted with saplings.

The last of this selection of graduate projects is located within the medieval church of St Olave's on Hart Street in the City of London. In 2004 the church commissioners were required to remove a precarious lime tree from the courtyard. As a consequence, efflorescence that had been kept at bay for decades gradually overcame the crypt's vaults. Ryan Martin's non-intrusive instruments imagined the crypt's original frescoed condition. Induced by friction and gravity, they scraped the vaulted ceiling of salts at an imperceptible pace to the eye. Residue was channelled through a series of glass pipettes, depositing a new 'projected fresco' on the crypt floor.

Each of these hypotheses argues that an intimate understanding of the physical and tactile cannot be reduced to a subordinate or indeed latter role in designing buildings. Far from it, such expertise and curiosity in the physical and tactile is central to the holistic scope of the designer's imagination.

I finish with a brief update on work in progress by sixteen*(makers), the group formed with my colleagues Phil Ayres, Chris Leung and Nick Callicott. For a number of years we have been 'in residence' at Kielder Forest in Northumbria. As many architectural actions begin, the residency has been approached as a survey. But rather than carry it out as a conventional geometric exercise, we have explored how the unique conditions that make up this landscape inform what kind of survey

it should be. Subsequently, the work we developed explored what was specific about this place, and how these conditions might define terms for architecture within this setting. We designed bespoke surveying tools to monitor and respond to local environmental behaviours, and installed them on a test site chosen for its remoteness as well as for its variety, adjacent to an area of dense forestation, an area recently harvested, and an area planted with saplings. The probes were designed to measure difference over time rather than the static characteristics of any given instance. Powered by solar energy, they logged and stored micro-environmental data in conditions that were often robust, occasionally serene and always variable. The probes were responsive to these changes, opening out when warm and sunny, closing down when cold and dark. The survey generated a resource for us which ordinarily would not be available to a designer, and this has been used to synthesise three issues: how surveys become active tools in making design decisions; how micro-environmental conditions may inform site selection; and how scope and variability in micro-environmental conditions may drive passively activated responsive behaviour all year round. Sixteen* makers have since been commissioned to design a small shelter by the reservoir at Kielder which is due for completion in 2009. **∆**

Note
1. R Sheil, 'Transgression from drawing to making', *Architectural Research Quarterly*, February 2006.

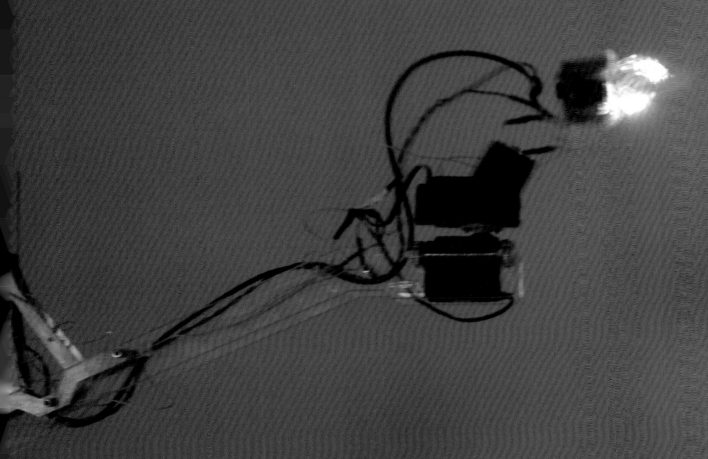

The Wonder of
Trivial Machines

Ruairi Glynn, Performative Ecologies, London,
Graz, Vienna and São Paulo, 2007–08

Having arrived in the 21st century at a definition of architecture that is time-based and responsive to the user, **Stephen Gage** finds 'reliable conceptual tools that can be used to understand our craft' wanting. He looks across to the rich seam of postwar cybernetics for inspiration. Drawing, in particular, on Heinz von Foerster's metaphor of the 'trivial machine', he urges us to transcend the reality of the predictable, creating the wonder and joy that is essential to architecture, through a dynamic relationship with context.

The discipline of cybernetics developed through the creation of goal-seeking control systems in autonomous and semi-autonomous machines during the Second World War. Early concepts were then used to understand control systems in biology and in human society. Architects, notably Nick Negroponte in the US and Cedric Price in the UK, were to become very interested in these concepts in the early 1960s.

The early cyberneticians made a distinction between a control system and the system that was being controlled. However, this distinction was effectively demolished in 1973 by the biologists Francisco Varela and Humberto Maturana, who presented the concept of autopoiesis, a self-defining living system with its goal embedded in it. A more general approach to systems using these ideas was enthusiastically adopted by a number of prominent cyberneticians and was called second-order cybernetics, or the cybernetics of cybernetics.

Once we consider architecture to be time based and enmeshed with the way that people perceive and use it, we find ourselves short of reliable conceptual tools that can be used to understand our craft. As an event or series of events in time, we can consider architecture as a performance containing both human and non-human changing protagonists. Some very old ideas may be re-examined to assist us in the huge range of possibilities on offer here.

Karl Normanton and Ian Laurence, The Graduation Ceremony, Diploma Unit 14, Bartlett School of Architecture, UCL, London, 2006
This 'costume' is one of seven prepared for a ritual engagement between the university faculties.

Trivial and Non-Trivial Machines

In his collection of papers and lectures entitled *Understanding Understanding*, one of the great second-order cyberneticians, Heinz von Foerster, developed the metaphor of a 'trivial machine' in which there are two definitions that sit inside each other:

A An explanation of external reality, which works every time.
B A thing with predictable behaviour in the external reality.

Heinz von Foerster's trivial machine.

In von Foerster's terms, B is an embodiment of A. He suggests that all of the machines that we construct and buy are trivial machines. We are surrounded by machines of this nature (toasters, dishwashers and so on), and our search for devices that allow us to create buildings that do not require the use of fossil fuels inevitably leads to the investigation of strange and unusual devices such as Nick Browne's The Fleas Knee – Nocturnal Ventilator.

Another way of describing a trivial machine is to treat it as a black box. Ranulph Glanville is both a design theorist and a cybernetician. He describes how y=(f) x is a description of a construct, of what exists inside a black box. The trivial machines that are designed and made can be thought of as constructed constructs, which may exist in black boxes. Glanville argues that our description of a black box is always tentative and potentially subject to change. The mental representation of a physically constructed construct can be a trivial machine to the designer and a black box to the user at the same time. In von Foerster's non-trivial machine, the inner element is invisible and the product (f) z is dependent on an internal feedback loop. The output continually varies, rather like the output from a chaos pendulum.

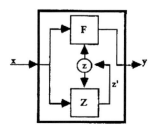

Heinz von Foerster's non-trivial machine.

Nick Browne, The Flea's Knee – Nocturnal Ventilator, Diploma Unit 14, Bartlett School of Architecture, UCL, London, 2005
This unusual device is an inscrutable object that does not have obvious functionality. So how do we begin to know what it does?

The mental representation of a physically constructed construct can be a trivial machine to the designer and a black box to the user at the same time.

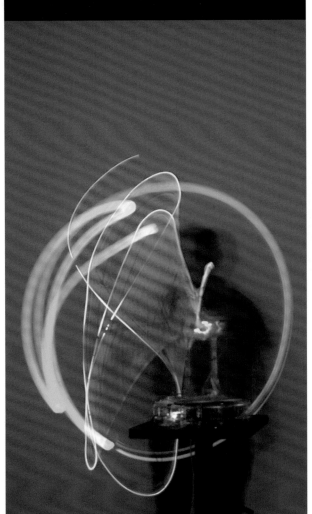

**Adam Somlai-Fischer,
Reorient – Migrating
Architectures, Hungarian
Pavilion, Venice
Architecture Biennale, 2006**
Architecture of delight:
Somlai-Fischer's assemblies
of children's toys delight
most of us as we recognise
their origins. We relearn how
they work as they interact
with each other and their
observers.

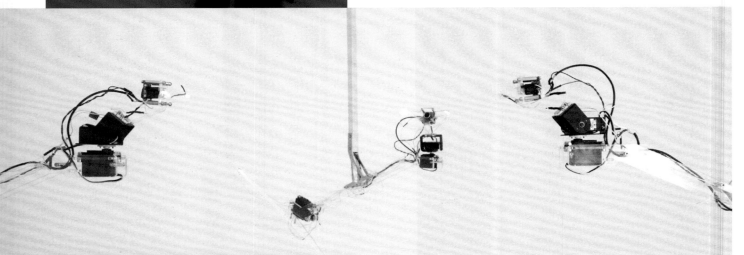

**Ruairi Glynn, Performative Ecologies, London, Graz, Vienna and
São Paulo, 2007–08**
Architecture of surprise: Ruairi Glynn's constantly evolving community
of 'dancers' improvise performances and evaluate the facial reactions
of people observing them. Using genetic algorithms they begin to
learn how best to please their audiences.

Delight and Surprise

Architecture is differentiated from building in that it is deemed to induce sensations of delight or wonder in its observers. The question that arises here is: where does this delight or wonder reside? By von Foerster's definition, a work of architecture is the physical embodiment of a trivial machine (a constructed construct). However, the process of constructing such a machine for the first time is not trivial and can induce sensations of delight. This applies both to the person who designs the machine (the architect) and to the observer who passes by and who reconstructs it in his or her own understanding. The interaction between the designer and the passer-by can be minimal, with the former having only a very primitive understanding of the latter.

Initial delight and wonder can pall. A further question that arises, therefore, is: can trivial or non-trivial machines be constructed so that the output is continually surprising and new? Simple ways of achieving this might be derived from time-based media, especially dynamic sculpture and performance art. Both of these examples rely on essentially predictable processes. By placing the constructed construct in the context of a wider changing environment and treating the output of the system as deriving from both, less predictable outputs can be achieved. In von Foerster's terms, when a trivial machine is nested inside another machine whose function is not fully known, the result is an inverted, non-trivial machine.

Harriet Lee, The Fire Pit, Diploma Unit 14, Bartlett School of Architecture, UCL, London, 2007
Harriet Lee shows, in an exquisite melding of the 'natural' and the 'artificial'; how a construct can evoke a sense of mystery and grace.

The architectural concept of delight comes indirectly from the Roman architect Vitruvius, who provides the earliest written account of the practice of architecture remaining to us. The 17th-century English poet Sir Henry Wootton wrote a commentary on Vitruvius's *Ten Books on Architecture* (*De Architectura*) in *The Elements of Architecture* he claims that every work of architecture should have the qualities of 'Firmness, Commodity and Delight'. This can be loosely translated as structural stability (and durability), usefulness and delight (or wonder). It is worth examining these attributes more closely. When we ascribe the quality of *firmness* to an object, we do this in terms of our understanding of the environment in which it sits. When we ascribe the quality of *commodity* to the same object we extend the description of the environment to include our understanding of the behaviour of people. When we go further and ascribe the quality of *delight* to an object, we can only do this in terms of our own understanding of the object or in terms of our understanding of the understanding of others.

Natural Magic

Von Foerster expresses a dislike of trivial machines and an admiration of non-trivial machines. He argues that trivial machines trivialise experience, especially the experience of communication. In this case, how do we explain his paper 'On Natural Magic', in which he describes how, as a youth, he was attracted to the machinery of performance (trivial machines) while his cousin was attracted to the performance of performance? He describes how he yearned for Weigleb's textbook *An Introduction to Natural Magic*, which would tell him how to make cheese, prepare wine, make Aeolian harps, project pictures on to the wall and so on.

Designers

An effective cheese-making machine is in the same class as an effective toaster. It is possible to make such a thing without directly considering the delight or wonder that the user might find in it despite how he or she may nevertheless experience delight when using it. Has this happened unintentionally, or is the designer relying on some other process? An approach where the creator of an artefact or performance excludes an in-depth consideration of the audience also lies at the heart of much contemporary art practice. The clues must lie both in the creators and in the observers of these constructed constructs.

The creators of this type of constructed construct usually know a lot about themselves. This approach can be summarised along the lines of 'if it interests me, then it will probably interest them', or, more usually, 'if it interests us, it will probably interest them' and if it delights us, it will probably delight them'. There are obvious pitfalls in this approach. On the other hand, work of this nature is never patronising and can be highly original, such as Harriet Lee's Fire Pit. Possible constructs are discussed and sketched and are modified through an iterative process of making and testing. The actual outcome can never be described at the start of the process. The design and creation of a constructed construct is the result of a conversation.

Conversations

Art and design practice, or 'praxis', is often represented in the form of different conversations. It is useful, in this context, to refer back to the master of conversation, Gordon Pask, who has remained a profound influence on many generations of architects through his long-standing relationship with the Architectural Association School of Architecture in London. Pask's work on the central necessity and the structure of conversation was framed in the context of learning systems. It derived from a concern about representation when sharing or learning singular concepts and became, in Pask's explorations, ever more general in its ramifications.

When Pask deals with physical architecture, he treats architecture as a knowledge structure (the traffic of which is the sharing of meaning between the designer and the public), which is open to epistemological consideration. In the context of the making of architecture, this is probably an overoptimistic assumption. Pask assumes that the designer wants to communicate with the public. It is quite possible to produce architectures where (except in the most banal sense) this is not the case. It is, however, vital that an architect communicates with him- or herself or, if he or she is in a large team, with fellow members of the design team. All buildings are embodiments of a mesh of interlinked concepts or interlinked topics. These concepts cannot successfully exist in isolation, and describe physically interdependent systems. To this extent, a building in gestation is an autogenetic entity fulfilling many of the criteria of a living system.

Gordon Pask, *c.* 1958. Gordon Pask and Cedric Price were instrumental in bringing cybernetics to the Architectural Association in the 1960s where they were a formative influence on a whole generation of students. Pask subsequently taught at the Architectural Association with John Fraser.

All buildings are embodiments of a mesh of interlinked concepts or interlinked topics. These concepts cannot successfully exist in isolation, and describe physically interdependent systems. To this extent, a building in gestation is an autogenetic entity fulfilling many of the criteria of a living system.

Passing Observers

What of the passing observers in this? When they approach a constructed construct for the first time they perceive it as a black box. Von Foerster's trivial machines are descriptions that use diagrams, mathematical notation and natural language. Constructed constructs often arrive with similar documents: these are called instruction manuals. In much the same way, art galleries increasingly use extended texts to describe the work on the wall. Instruction manuals are useful when they offer observers an insight into the way that a constructed construct might be used or maintained. It is possible that they might offer a route to a sense of wonder and delight in the usefulness and cleverness of the artefact. It is far harder to imagine how an instruction manual could, except in a very general way, assist observers when they look at the constructed construct as a whole and find wonder and delight in it. Until relatively recently, the majority of the population could not read manuals. Regardless of this, the earliest human artefacts show evidence of attempts to play with delight and wonder, usually through the use of particular shapes and patterns.

In his Interactive Acoustic Feedback installation, Richard Roberts uses human presence and the reconfiguration of space to modify a self-generated analogue acoustic output. The spectral music that results can be experienced by two classes of observer: the person who is instrumental in changing the acoustic architecture, and those who observe the transformation from a distance. In both cases, the specific transformations have to be learnt before they can be enjoyed. Glanville argues that it is the making of pattern and coherence in things that leads us to a sense of wonder and delight. This sense of wonder can occur both when we design and construct a physical construct, and when we observe one for the first time and construct it for ourselves by seeing a pattern within it. This sense of wonder is founded in the way that we perceive the world.

Learning

Von Foerster also argues that the world that we see is the world that we have constructed in our minds. He claims that this world is learnt. A substantial body of work that supports this view is emerging in the field of perceptual science, notably the ground-breaking work of Richard Gregory at the Department of Experimental Psychology, University of Bristol. Perception, learning and memory are intertwined and feed back on each other. It is the process of learning that makes the journey to a new place always longer than the journey back.

Unlike amphibians, we arrive in our world with very little prior knowledge of it. This allows us to learn and to take advantage of a vast range of environments and experiences. We are driven by curiosity, fear and, because we are social animals an urge to copy. Our urge is to construct relationships and to recognise patterns, and it extends to finding them when they do not exist, as we look for them in many different processes and objects. Von Foerster argues that the learner usually constructs an understanding that creates or re-creates a trivial machine. This is not trivial for the learner – it can be deeply satisfying and sometimes transcendentally beautiful. This is the wonder that Glanville refers to. Learning can lead to an epiphany of understanding – and this can lead to a sense of wonder.

> The most beautiful thing we can experience is the mysterious.
> Albert Einstein, *The World As I See It*, 1932

But what happens when the observers have learnt the constructed construct, when the trivial machine has been made? Does the wonder cease? Glanville argues that if the constructed construct leads to introspection, then the wonder never ceases. This said, the answer is probably yes in many cases. Certainly, Pask speculates that without variety an observer will become disinterested. Perhaps if the variety is great enough the observer will always learn new things – a continuous epiphany.

Richard Roberts, Interactive Acoustic Feedback, Diploma Unit 14, Bartlett School of Architecture, UCL, London, 2007
In this haunting and space-specific acoustic installation, the sound is modified by a member of the audience who becomes part of a performance for other observers.

Continual Delight

One way of looking to achieve continual delight is to refer to those art forms that continuously offer variety to the observer. These are time based, and usually involve performance in one form or another. Architecture has always provided a backdrop for social ritual and performance, and architects (notably Inigo Jones) have investigated social performance directly through the creation of settings and costume. More recently, Karl Normanton and Ian Laurence have shown in The Graduation Ceremony how the structure of an institution and the nature of its iconic architecture can be exposed to observers through the use of massive dance prostheses. A performance is a class of physically constructed construct where the physicality of the experience is inevitably ephemeral. Can a physical object be imbued with this capability?

The moves of an automaton can, like the melody of a piece of music, be learnt. Both are then predictable. Is it possible to envisage constructed constructs that can show outputs that have pattern and are unpredictable? Is it possible to construct a wide range of physical devices that behave like von Foerster's non-trivial machine, where an output is a form of pattern that continually changes but remains strangely familiar?

Another way of creating variety is to extend the boundary of the constructed construct so that the boundary around it includes some of the environment in which the construct sits. This can work well if there is any form of complexity in the wider environment. The work of Fred Guttfield shows how simple environmental reactions can be used to construct complex patterns of interaction when linked to an object with a simple memory. His Second Order Bird Feeder remembers its interaction with the birds that feed from it, and plays these back when there are no birds present. Of course, the result is strangely familiar to any birds that are passing by.

An obvious environment for architects to work with is the natural world that von Foerster found to be so magical. There are, in architecture, historical examples of this. In these, the effect is passive in that the architecture is a fixed element in a wider dynamic system. The best known, in the UK, is the ancient stone circle at Stonehenge in Wiltshire. The constructed construct is a complex sundial and is still a place of meeting used to celebrate the dawn on midsummer's day. It is easy to understand how a trivial machine could be made out of this – in the Sahara Desert. The UK has some of the most unpredictable weather in the world, especially during a British summer. Waiting for the sun to rise in a predictable position on a predictable day has

a sense of awe and majesty about it. Waiting and wondering whether there will be a sun to see at the appointed time introduces a high level of uncertainty to the proceedings.

Two common threads run through this type of work. First, the designer/artist tries to take on a role that is similar to that of a traditional scientist. He or she maintains a distance from the final outcome, because the effect of the work on people (excluding the designer) is not central to its production. Second, architectural constructed constructs are placed in unpredictable external environments and invert von Foerster's general proposition. They consist of trivial machines that become non-trivial by virtue of changes in an outer state.

Von Foerster describes a non-trivial machine as a trivial machine with a further, unknown machine inside it that modifies the output in an unpredictable way. He writes extensively about the variety that can be generated through hidden 'inner states'. Architectural trivial machines become black boxes that nest in larger black boxes that affect their perceived outputs in unpredictable ways. This is how a trivial machine can be observed in delight and wonder again and again by designers and passing observers alike. Some physical architecture has been designed in this way for millions of years, with the assumption that the physical stuff of architecture is static. Recent attempts in the same area include physical constructs that shade and

Karl Normanton and Ian Laurence, The Graduation Ceremony, Diploma Unit 14, Bartlett School of Architecture, UCL, London, 2006
The structure of an institution and the nature of its iconic architecture are here exposed to observers through the use of massive dance prostheses.

reflect daylight and sunlight according to the time of day, time of year and the state of the weather. And more complex, active (as opposed to passive) constructed constructs can also be placed back in 'natural' conditions. This approach leads the designer to a new understanding of the importance of context. Dynamic context is not something to be respected, it is something to be utilised and enjoyed as an integral part of the finished work. ⚫

Fred Guttfield, Second Order Bird Feeder, Thames Valley, Diploma Unit 14, Bartlett School of Architecture, UCL, London, 2007
The Second Order Bird Feeder remembers the oscillations that the birds have induced and plays these back to them; it also plays the memory of the birds to people when the birds are away.

Bibliography
GM Boyd and G Pask, 'Why do instructional designers need conversation theory?', in D Laurillard (ed), *Interactive Media: Working Methods and Practical Applications*, Ellis Horwood (Chichester), 1987.
A Einstein, *The World as I see it*, 1932. Retrieved 2 September 2005 from S Gage, 'Heinz Von Foerster is a member of the Viennese Magic Circle', *Architectural Design: Reflexive Architecture*, Vol 72, No 3, 2002, pp 80–8.
H von Foerster, 'On Natural Magic', in *Understanding Understanding: Essays on Cybernetics and Cognition*, Springer-Verlag (New York), 2002.
R Glanville, 'Inside every white box there are two black boxes trying to get out', *Behavioural Science*, Vol 12, 1982.
R Glanville, 'Machines of wonder and elephants that float in the air', *Cybernetics and Human Knowing*, Vol 10, Nos 3–4, 2003, pp 91–106.
R Goldberg, 'Space as praxis', *Studio International*, Vol 191, No 978, 1975.
RL Gregory, *Eye and Brain: The Psychology of Seeing*, Oxford University Press (Oxford), 1997.
GS Hawkins and JB White, *Stonehenge Decoded*, Souvenir Press (London), 1972.
JY Lettvin, HR Maturana, WS Mcculloch and WH Pitts, *What the Frog's Eye Tells the Frog's Brain*, 1959. Retrieved 2 September 2005 from http://jerome.lettvin.info/WhatTheFrogsEyeTellsTheFrogsBrain.pdf.
MH Morgan, *Vitruvius: The Ten Books on Architecture*, trans MH Morgan, Dover Publications (New York), 1960.
G Pask, 'A comment, a case history and a plan', in J Reichardt (ed), *Cybernetics, Art and Ideas*, Graphic Society Ltd and Studio Vista (Greenwich, NY, and London), 1971.
D Purves and R Beau Lotto, *Why We See What We Do: An Empirical Theory of Vision*, Sinauer Associates Inc (Sunderland, MA), 2003.

Architectural trivial machines become black boxes that nest in larger black boxes that affect their perceived outputs in unpredictable ways. This is how a trivial machine can be observed in delight and wonder again and again by designers and passing observers alike.

Strandbeests

Theo Jansen, **Animaris Percipiere, Ijmuiden, The Netherlands, May 2005** Animaris Percipiere (morning).

Dutch artist **Theo Jansen** has created his own genesis, raising fantastic beasts out of plastic tubing. Photographed on the beach near his lab in Ypenburg, these great sculptures have a mythical resonance far beyond their physical make-up. Here he explains the inherent qualities and restrictions of working with this ubiquitous yellow electric cabling that lends itself to playful experiment and accidental evolutions.

Animaris Percediere (evening)

In Germany they have grey plastic tubes, in America they make them of metal. Every country has its own kind of tube. Today, Dutch plastic tubing is yellow. In the late 1940s the insulation used for electric cabling was nowhere near as satisfactory as it is today, so it was decreed in the Netherlands in 1947 that all electric wiring must be encased in plastic tubing (or conduit as it is known in the UK). The country has produced something like 6 million kilometres (3.7 million miles) of tubing since then. It can be found among rubble in skips, tied to the roof racks of delivery vans, or lying about in the street. In the 1980s Dutch manufacturers changed the colour of the tubing from white to the yellowish hue it still has today.

I first used tubing as early as 1979 to make a flying saucer that flew over Delft and caused a near riot. Hula hoops were made from this tubing in the 1960s, and it was also popular among kids who used it to make blowpipes for firing paper darts with messages on them. The mere possibility of this form of airmail delivery fascinated me.

Exposure to sun and rain causes the current yellow tubing to fade to the same white it once was. It also becomes brittle and bone-like with time. In the beach animal boneyard at my lab in Ypenburg near The Hague, fossils of extinct species can be seen bleaching in the sun. Their age can be estimated from their colour.

In the Netherlands, plastic tubing costs 10 eurocents a metre, which means that a large beach animal 10 metres (32.8 feet) long, 4 metres (13.1 feet) wide and 4 metres (13.1 feet) high uses about 100 euros of tubing. The first obstacle on the path to artificial life was the problem of connecting the tubes: how were they to be fastened together? I started by sawing pieces of tube and winding adhesive tape around their extremities. Out of this first means of fastening came the first beach animal: Animaris Vulgaris. This adhesive tape period was brief, lasting only a year.

We know that nature consists largely of protein. I, too, want to make my own life forms from a single material. You can use protein to make skin, eyes, lungs. Protein is multipurpose stuff. And so is tubing. It is flexible, but exceedingly rigid when used in a triangular construction. You can run pistons through it, store air in it, all sorts. I only discovered the wide range of its uses after many peregrinations through what I call 'being-able' country. Given the restrictions of this

Animaris Percipiere (sea foam).

Animaris Rhinoceros

Animaris Percipiere (sea foam 2).

Animaris Percipiere (storm).

Animaris Percipiere (storm 2).

Test components and joints in yellow plastic tubing.

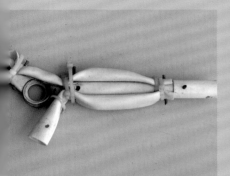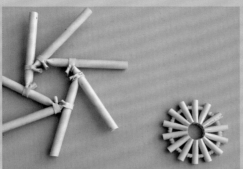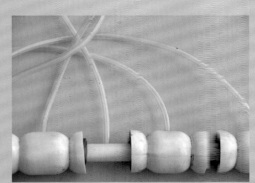

material, I was forced to seek out escape routes that were neither logical nor obvious. The strategy I followed is the reverse of that taken by an engineer.

Suppose that engineers at a university of technology were to be commissioned to make something that could move of its own volition along the beach. What would you expect them to do? You can bet your life they would respond in months and also that they would have assembled stainless-steel robot-like devices armed with sensors, cameras and light cells. Devices that are first thought out and then assembled. That is how engineers work. They have ideas and then they make the ideas happen. First they pore over books, then they open all the drawers in their workplace and take out what they need. It is a working method that, no two ways about it, gives rapid and reliable results.

However, the idea for the beach animals was not determined this way. They evolved from an accident after I had been fooling around with plastic tubes for quite some time. It was as though the beach animals led me to make them by sheer chance. Remarkably, chance is more likely to play a role when there are restrictions. Financial restrictions, for example, may mean that drawers in the workplace stay closed. This necessitates looking for other possibilities elsewhere. During this search, new ideas automatically emerge, ideas that are often better than the ones you first had.

Searching and fooling around is a long way of going about things; your destination has yet to be decided. You park your car along the hard shoulder and scramble down the bank, machete in hand, hacking a path through the undergrowth. You will probably never arrive at a destination in the accepted sense of the word, but you are very likely to call in at places no one has ever been before. What is handy about this method is that found materials are made to devise or invent.

Though I did my best to escape nature, I could not avoid resorting to its principles at times.

One occasion was when I was developing new legs for the Strandbeests. I could find no better, energy-efficient device for perambulating across sandy surfaces than those already in existence. I do not think there is anything that can beat good old legs. Now I am working on muscles, nerves, brains. I was not looking for them, but they happen to come in handy if you wish to survive on the beach. Survival is also reliant on food, defence and reproduction. The food of Strandbeests is wind. They get their camouflage from sand clinging to the adhesive tape (Animaris Sabulosa), and they reproduce by cannibalism (Animaris Geneticus).

I take comfort in the thought that these parallels have occurred in biological evolution. Consider the fish and the dolphin. They are unrelated. But as we know, the dolphin is a mammal, the fish is a fish, and yet they still have more or less the same shape. Evidently nature could not come up with an aquadynamic form other than that of the fish: fattish at the front and gradually narrowing to a point at the tail. I have come to empathise with creators such as this not just in the tussle with stuff, but also in the sheer pleasure of evolving and making. You cannot imagine the excitement that possesses me when something works, even though it may be a mere detail. ∆

Drawn into Space

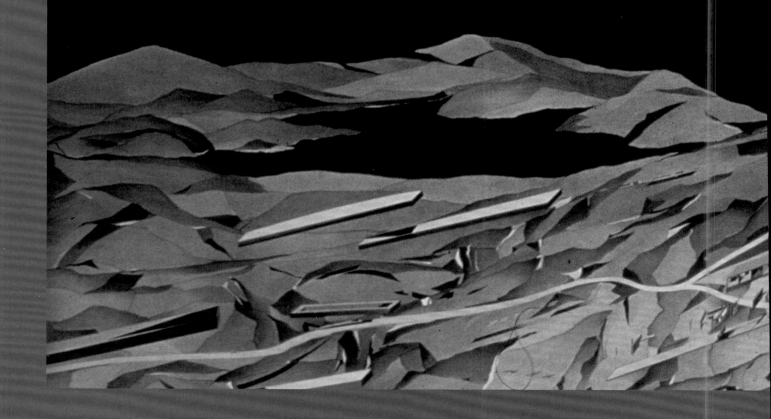

Zaha Hadid

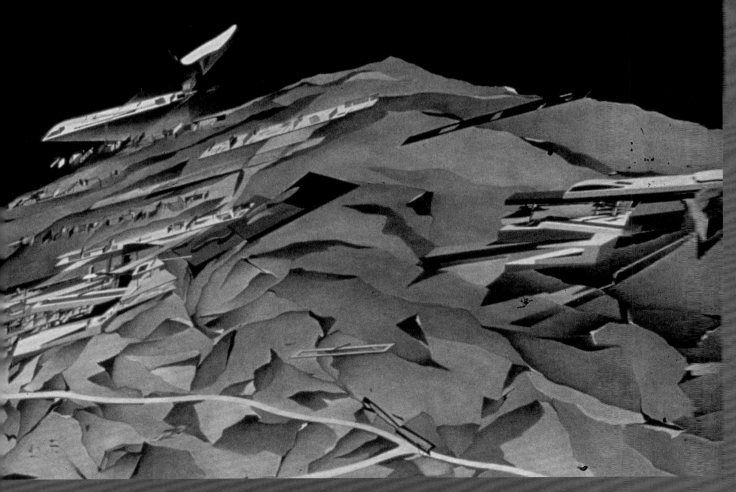

The Peak, Hong Kong, 1982–3

Visionary New York architect **Lebbeus Woods** reviews the evolution of Zaha Hadid's work from the 1970s to the present. Tracking the shifts in her work from a Suprematist-informed fragmentation in the 1980s to a more contemporary fluidity and a preoccupation with complex curvilinearity, he throws light on the relationship between Hadid's drawing and her architecture.

When I first visited Zaha Hadid's small studio in 1984, I saw a watercolour she was working on taped to a drawing board. It was a delicate and intricate drawing related to her breakthrough project for The Peak, Hong Kong, of 1982–3. Being one who drew, I asked her what brushes she used. Red sable? Without a comment, she showed me a cheap paint-trim 'brush' that can be bought at any corner hardware store – a wedge of grey foam on a stick. I still remember being shocked into silence. Years later, I came to understand her choice of tools as characteristic of her approach to architecture: a wringing of the extraordinary out of the mundane.

From the beginning of her creative work, Hadid has used drawing, to an unusual degree, as a means of visualising her architectural ideas. Her way of drawing has changed over the years as her practice has changed, from that of a radical visionary – a reference most commonly applied to those who do not build – to an architect designing large-scale projects that are now being built in various parts of the world. My primary interest here is the evolution of her drawings and how they have affected the concepts of her architecture.

Most architects make drawings. However, Hadid's drawings of the 1980s are different, and in several ways. Most notably she had to originate new systems of projection in order to formulate in spatial terms her complex thoughts about architectural forms and the relationships between them. These new projection methods were widely copied in their time, and influenced the then-nascent computer-modelling culture. More to the point, they enabled her to synthesise entire landscapes within which a project she was designing may have been only a small part. This has been crucial to her thought because she sees architecture as an integral part of the wider world. She was a global architect long before the term acquired its present meaning.

There is another way in which these drawings are not only unique, but uniquely important to Hadid's idea of architecture: they must carry the entire weight of her intellectual investment. Her written statements about the work are, frankly, blandly descriptive, betraying little of her philosophy and even less of her aspiration to employ her architecture as a unifying force in the world. Her lectures, while getting a boost from her charisma, are no more revealing. But her drawings speak volumes about her outlook, her intellectual depth, and her ambition to place architecture at the dynamic centre of an ever more dynamic world.

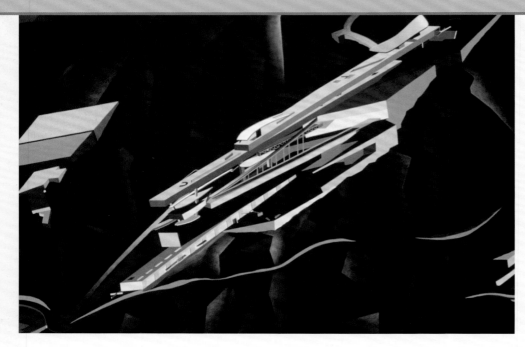

The Peak, Hong Kong, 1982–3

Her detractors have often said Hadid's drawings are only about style, ignoring their systematic and obsessively analytical construction. On close examination, we find that the drawings reveal complex and subtle rearrangements and reinterpretations of what most of us would call reality, portraying new forms of spatial order governing the relationships between sky and earth, horizon and ground, the artificial and the natural. Her drawings for the Grand Buildings in Trafalgar Square, London, project of 1985 exploit ideas of scale to make London a tabula rasa for a brave, new Hadidian world. The seminal Peak drawings fragment both architecture and the mountainside overlooking Hong Kong, allowing them to intermingle in a startling, seemingly natural synthesis. Who else had dared such reconstructions of the familiar and the venerable? Bruno Taut, in his *Alpine Architecture*? Le Corbusier, in his *Radiant City*? Perhaps, but never in the context of projects so intended to be realised. This work was serious theory in visual form, and more. The drawings were manifestoes of a new architecture that Hadid was clearly determined to realise in building, and against any odds.

Hadid's work of the 1980s was paradoxical. From one perspective, it seemed to be a Postmodern effort to strike out in a new direction by appropriating the tectonic languages of an earlier epoch – notably Russian avant-garde at the time of the revolution – but in a purely visual, imagistic way: the political and social baggage had been discarded. This gave her work an uncanny effect. The drawings and the architecture they depicted were powerfully asserting something, but just what the something was, in traditional terms, was unclear. However, from another perspective this work seemed strongly rooted in Modernist ideals: its obvious mission was to reform the world through architecture. Such an all-encompassing vision had not been seen since the 1920s. Hadid alluded to this when she spoke about 'the unfinished project' of Modernism that she clearly saw her work carrying forward. With this attitude she fell into the anti-Postmodern (hardly popular) camp championed by Jürgen Habermas. Understandably, people were confused about what to think, but one thing was certain: what they saw looked amazing, fresh and original, and was an instant sensation.

Studying the drawings from this period, we find that fragmentation is the key. Animated bits and pieces of buildings and landscapes fly through the air. The world is changing. It breaks up, scatters and reassembles in unexpectedly new, yet uncannily familiar forms. These are the forms of buildings, of cities, places we are meant to inhabit, clearly in some new ways, though we are never told how. We must be clever enough, or inventive

enough, to figure it out for ourselves: the architect gives no explicit instructions, except in the drawings. Maybe we too, must psychically fragment, scatter and reassemble in unexpected new configurations of thinking and living. Or, maybe the world, in its turbulence and unpredictability, has already pushed us in this direction.

It is useful to recall at this point that Modernism in architecture had two competing directions. One, prominently represented by the Bauhaus, aimed at redesigning the world in conformance with the demands of industrialisation, including its social dimensions, such as workers' housing. The other, represented by De Stijl and the Russian avant-garde, aimed at a transformation of spirit and the creation of a new society taking radical forms of every kind. Of the latter, we can think of Tatlin, Leonidov and Malevich. Malevich was primarily a painter and the creator of the Suprematist movement, which emphasised abstraction as an almost religious mode of spiritual change. Of the two Modernist directions, Hadid was strongly attached to Suprematism. Her thesis project at the Architectural Association in the 1970s, under the tutelage of Rem Koolhaas, took one of Malevich's seminal tektonics as a starting point. Placing it along and across the Thames in central London, she left no doubt, to the cognoscenti at least, as to her ideological position: she was reviving a neglected, almost stillborn Modernist ideal and reasserting it into the contemporary world.

But why?

Malevich's Tektonic, London, 1977

It is, of course, interesting to speculate on the reason why Hadid used Malevich as her starting point. She has never written or publicly spoken about it. In private, she is evasive about the subject. Koolhaas' own preference was for the Constructivists, with their technological symbolism and collectivist social programmes more attuned to the culture of his native Holland. I believe that Hadid's reasons were personal, emerging from her life journey from Baghdad, through Beirut (where she majored in mathematics) and Switzerland to London. They are also cultural. Iraq is, after all, a descendant of the most ancient of civilisations, and its spiritual values predate religions such as Christianity and Islam, and modern ideas of nations and states. The transience of life, with its technological and social upheavals, pales before enduring philosophies. The abstractions and metaphysics of Suprematism have this character.

Fragmentation can be philosophical, too. It can be systematic and not merely chaotic or accidental. This can be seen in some of Malevich's earlier paintings. Or, even if it is chaotic, it can reflect an existentialist edge, a risky form of play with disintegration as a prelude or even an impetus to a higher re-formation. As long as forms remain whole, unified, coherent, they cannot be transformed. Only when established forms are broken up are they susceptible to change. This formal verity is a virtual metaphor for modern society: the break-up caused by political revolutions and new technological capabilities has created a human world not only susceptible to new forms, but demanding of them. Hadid's work, as manifest in her drawings, emerged at a time when there was much soul-searching among serious architects and theorists about the why and how of reformulating architecture in response to the changes overtaking society. Hadid's answer was like the blow of Alexander to the Gordian Knot: decisive, if nothing else. The battle was engaged.

It is well known that Hadid has had an unusually difficult time getting her projects built. The radical forms of The Peak, the Hafenstrasse Building in Hamburg (1990) and the Düsseldorf Art and Media Centre (1992/3), among others proposed during the 1980s, attracted developers who would have loved to capitalise on them, but in the end did not have the courage. It took a patron, Rolf Fehlbaum of Vitra, to actually build her first fully realised project, a fire station for his furniture factory in Weil am Rhein, Germany, in 1993. But by then her drawings were changing.

To put it simply, fragmentation began to give way to fluid form. The change was already evident in her drawings analysing the farming landscape around the Vitra factory site for the project, imparting a linear

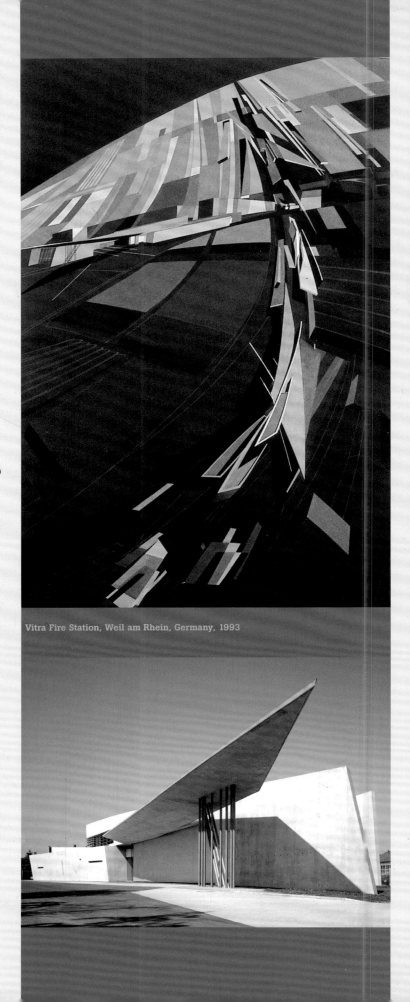

Vitra Fire Station, Weil am Rhein, Germany, 1993

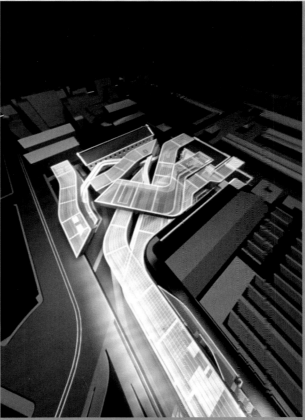

National Museum of XXI Century Arts, Rome, 1998–2008

dynamic that comes together in the powerful thrust of the little building. The vision here is no longer about breaking up and scattering. Rather, it is about gathering together and directing. It is also about the making of unified, and unifying, forms. As with other questions about which she has given no explanation or insight, we are left to puzzle out the reasons for this change in her drawings and the designs they describe.

It seems that there are two separate sets of possible reasons, not entirely conflicting. The first is that over the 10 years between The Peak and the Vitra Fire Station, Hadid's thinking had evolved in a natural way, following a trajectory from utopian visions of an ideal Hadidian world to Hadidian interpretations of the world as it actually is. The second is her gradual acceptance of the fact that, if she wanted to build, her designs would have to work within property lines and other limitations – material and conceptual – imposed by clients. Her buildings, in other words, would have to become more compact and contained, more unified and more buildable in the conventional sense of the term.

However, another factor, as fate would have it, impacted her development in the 1990s, and that was the growing pre-eminence of the computer in architectural design and construction. Not only architects, but clients, engineers and contractors expected to see computer drawings that could be read in exchanged between them and directly translated into the computer-aided manufacture of building elements. This development coincided with the dramatic shift in Hadid's designs, and clearly gave it impetus.

From the mid-1990s onwards, Hadid was increasingly interested in complexly curvilinear, fluid dynamic forms that can be drawn by conventional hand methods – with French curves and the like – but are much more quickly and accurately drawn using computer programs. She and her team, now grown from a small cadre to more than a hundred, were still producing hand paintings for projects such as the National Museum of XXI Century Arts in Rome (1998–2003) and the Rosenthal Center for Contemporary Art in Cincinnati, Ohio (2004), but these have the feel of being made for exhibition purposes and lack the pictorial vibrancy and conceptual urgency of earlier, exploratory paintings and drawings. The real action had moved to the computer. In one sense it liberated the architect, enabling her to create the unprecedented forms that have, by the present day, become her signature. In another, it brought an end to a certain intimacy and feel of tentative, almost hesitant expectancy in her drawings and designs that was part of the intense excitement they generated.

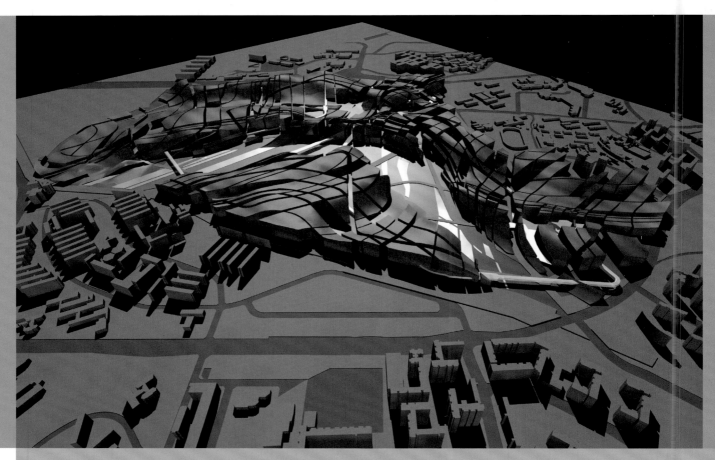

One North Masterplan, Singapore, 2001

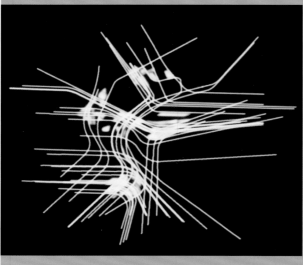

Whether she works on the computer in the direct way she once did with foam brushes I have no idea. Certainly, the new method of drawing has done nothing to diminish the intensity of her architecture, though it has changed it as a visual presence and a philosophical proposition. The forms gather energies around them and retain them. The contained energy contorts simple forms into complex ones. They are tightly wound, or bundled, and seem ready to explode – though they do not.

Today, Hadid's global vision includes urban planning projects for Singapore and Bilbao and, no doubt, others to come. The urban landscape, re-formed by her architecture, was always a basic theme of her work. In her earlier drawings and speculative urban projects, swarms of tectonic fragments accreted into Hadidian buildings, either among existing buildings – as in The Peak's Hong Kong – or on an abstract field of city blocks or other boundaries, as in The World (89 Degrees) of 1983. In the new designs, energy flows congeal into vaster urban sections, no longer mere buildings. This quantitative shift is also qualitative. It is one thing to imagine Hadid's buildings as anchors in a broadly diverse landscape, but it is quite another to imagine entire districts that must conform to her designs. Reminiscent of the approach of Baron Haussmann to 19th-century

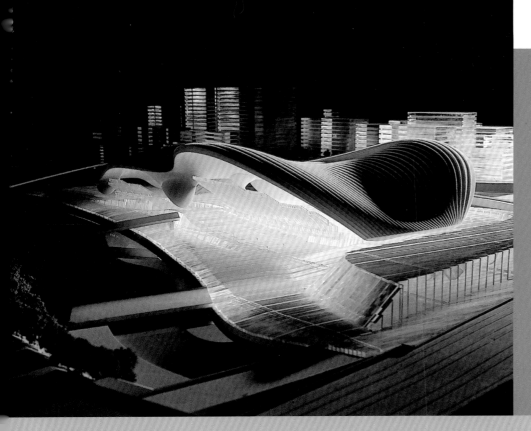

London Aquatics Centre, London, 2005

Paris, or of Robert Moses to 20th-century New York, these are imperial in scale and intent: a unification by big gestures that confirm some form of centralised state, or private, corporate power to make such gestures in the complex fabric of a city.

Fragmentation is inherently democratic, regardless of how dominated at any moment by one style or another: that, after all, remains a measure of choice. Big gestures, however elegant or effective they may be, are inherently autocratic. Here we stand at the precipitous divide between art and politics, which is exactly the domain of architecture in any age. It is the edge on which Hadid's drawings and projects are, at this moment, delicately poised.

The legacies of Mesopotamia and Suprematism both suggest the long view. Over the ages it is the architecture that matters, that will endure. It is the architecture that vindicates the human condition, not the other way round. The work of a great artist, or architect, always poses the most difficult questions. We look to Zaha Hadid's work for answers, and must wait and see. ⌀

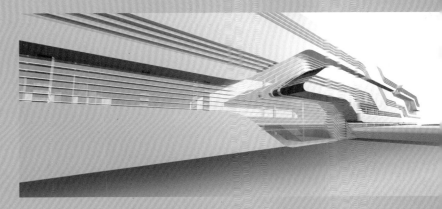

Pierre Vives, Montpellier, France, 2002–09

Guggenheim Museum, Taichung, Taiwan, 2003

Convoluted Flesh

A Synthetic Approach to Analogue and Digital Architecture

Marcos Cruz and Marjan Colletti advocate their own distinct design approach that is intuitive and blissful in its opulence, evoking the sublime. Here they discuss the potential of opening up 'new spatial, or material possibilities' that are liberated from the self-imposed restrictions of their more technologically driven contemporaries.

Sara Shafiei (Unit 20),
Anamorphic Tectonics, Rome,
2006–07

previous spread: Handcrafted
model of digitally modelled cone
surfaces for a magician's theatre.
The project convolutes structural
and stylistic design criteria,
understanding architecture in its
3-D depth and ornamented
richness. Within the flesh of
anamorphic tectonics, elephants
are made to disappear:
Houdini's favourite trick.

Marjan Colletti, *2&1/2D
(Twoandahalf Dimensionality,
#3 & #22, 2002–07*

right: 2&1/2D results from an
intuitive and playful interaction
with software packages in order
to express and mediate the
properties (rather than
parameters) of an interstitial,
floating, digital world
constituted by a plethora of
image/thing hybrids. These
2&1/2D constructs are not
illustrations of calculated
shapes, but expressions of
formulated circumstances. The
purely vector-based
(geometrically precise, yet
entirely abstract) drawings are
constructed in 2-D space (no z-
axis value, yet spatial depth)
and describe convoluted,
ornamented, 'splinear' fields
and blots rather than finite,
enclosed, surface-based objects
and blobs.

The convoluted (that is, overlapped, intertwined and
blurred) nature of contemporary architectural design
described here goes beyond the functions of opulence and
intricacy, of technique and simulation, of module and
optimisation. It invokes something ranking above notions
of beauty, style and elegance;[1] it evokes the sublime, the
blissful and the mysterious even within the digital domain.
The concept of Convoluted Flesh, which is central to the
design investigations of marcosandmarjan and their
Diploma Unit 20 at the Bartlett School of Architecture,
University College London, entails an organic spatial and
strategic vision that includes the significance of
atmospherics and bodily experience in conjunction with
the designer's technological and poetic awareness.

Simultaneously, the understanding of 'flesh'[2] in
architectural terms stands in opposition to the common,
yet reductive, metaphor of skin as a flat and thin
membrane that denies the virtue of inhabitable thick
walls. At a time when much of the mainstream digital
discourse is essentially surface-bound – risking flattening
and disembodying the architectural skin even more, and
at the same time depriving it of its human and material
content – the aim of Convoluted Flesh, on the contrary, is
to stress the urgency of a thick embodied flesh that
encompasses new ornamental, sensual and corporeal
qualities in architecture.

Consequently, the endeavour is to establish a debate in
which experimentation, technology and progress exclude

neither the intuitive and poetic freedom of designers as truly creative
thinkers, nor the inherent relationship between the user and the
depth of the architectural flesh. Hence a poetic, as well as a
'corpological', approach is considered that complements a
typological and topological understanding of architecture. Leading
debates in the digital realm are often still very much the result of an
initial period of discovery of disembodied virtual realities,
datascapes and cyber-realities that culminated in an almost quasi-
religious myth of total liberation from physical limitations. Such
processes, it seems, have focused more on generating architecture
from outside via formulated methodologies towards structural,
engineered tectonics. The notion of Convoluted Flesh, on the other
hand, implies an approach that develops from inside out, involving
experiential qualities, inhabitation and use. Rather than following
the structural 'truthful' efficiency of the Gothic and its parametric
revival, phenomena of Convoluted Flesh are intrinsically associated
with a sense of formal, structural and spatial complexity, borrowing
from a plethora of baroque binary conditions such as the dichotomy
of rational and empirical thinking, along with the morphing of
classical architectural semantics into playful theatrical tectonics and
typologies. It involves the body in a variety of arguments that aim for
the synthesis of techniques, technics and technologies,[3] and the
performance (understood both as task and as staging) of the
architectural flesh.

The professional and academic design research of
marcosandmarjan spirals away from the apparently unquestioned
and rather predictable version of what can be understood as the
contemporary emergence of a new 'digital modernism': the

Marcos Cruz, *Cyborgian Interfaces*, 1999–2007
left top and bottom:
In Cyborgian Interfaces, essential domestic functions such as sitting, sleeping or communicating are transferred from the traditional room-space into inhabitable appliance walls. It creates an exoskeleton that prompts a new haptic relationship between the body and its sensitive–reactive environment. Like an urban coral reef, the building facade and its exposed communication sleeves, tentacles and sitting bulges are understood as architectural flesh, creating a dynamic scenario of unprecedented character.

The aim of Convoluted Flesh . . . is to stress the urgency of a thick embodied flesh that encompasses new ornamental, sensual and corporeal qualities in architecture.

marcosandmarjan, El Coral, Museum for Iberian and South American Art (MEIAC), Badajoz, Spain, 2005–06
above: The proposal extends the existing museum with an ornamental canopy that feels like a large-scale urban coral. The structure is conceived as an environmental regulator that filters light and heat, as well as embedding numerous services such as kiosks, ticket offices, shops and gallery spaces

marcosandmarjan, Nurbster I and VI, London/Prague and Hamburg, 2004, 2005
The Nurbsters employ a file-to-factory design methodology that finds possible applications in experimental timber and steel structures, facades, canopies, ornamental surfaces and ergonomic internal secondary structures, division walls and furniture pieces. Furthermore, they react to sustainable issues by optimising the layout of the positive cut-outs on the boards and by reusing the negative cut-outs as ornamental dividing screens.

BY LOOKING INTO ADVANCES WITHIN A WIDE RANGE OF MANUFACTURING TECHNOLOGIES AND WORKING METHODOLOGIES, ALL PROPOSED WORK AIMS FOR AN OPEN-MINDED AND CREATIVE INTERPRETATION OF SUCH PROCESSES, SIMULTANEOUSLY PURSUING A SYNTHETIC MODEL OF DESIGN THAT CONVOLUTES THE TECHNOLOGICAL WITH THE POETIC, THE VISIONARY WITH THE HISTORIC, AS WELL AS THE ORNAMENTAL AND TECTONIC WITHIN THE ARCHITECTURAL FLESH

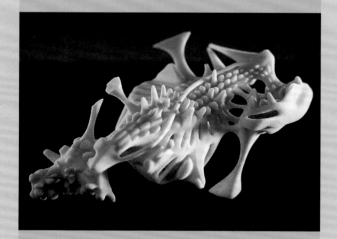

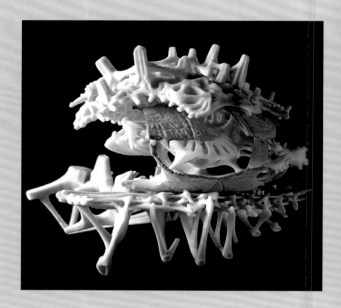

Tobias Klein (Unit 20), Synthetic Syncretism, Havana, 2005–06
Hybrid Relic – The Chelonian Urne: The project revolves around the construction of a series of sacrificial utensils that suit possible rituals of the Cuban syncretic religion of Santeria, which combines elements of African and Catholic beliefs. 3-D scanned and 3-D rapid-prototyped, these relics hybridise real and artificial bones in a process that is surgically precise, yet magically inventive.

unspecified whitewash (or often just 'greywash') of 3-D surfaces, the universal *Sachlichkeit* (objectiveness) of parametric design techniques, and the mechanistic concept of the computer as a purely generative utensil. In turn, different notions of Convoluted Flesh challenge such approaches, envisioning experimental and thus unpredictable conditions in design that are the result of the individual's eccentric yet informed understanding of architecture. By looking into advances within a wide range of manufacturing technologies and working methodologies, all proposed work aims for an open-minded and creative interpretation of such processes, simultaneously pursuing a synthetic model of design that convolutes the technological with the poetic, the visionary with the historic, as well as the ornamental and tectonic within the architectural flesh.

An example of this is the Nurbster series, which combines models and 1:1 prototypes conceived as exhibition installations, and their implications on larger-scale constructs. They create an analogue/digital repertoire by utilising 2-D/3-D modelling software, in addition to CNC, CAD/CAM and rapid prototyping technologies that allow the easy assemblage of a large amount of components. The size and scale of the majority of Nurbsters locates them within the domain of interior and urban furniture design, which considers modularity and mass production, structural stability and tectonic presence. The results are assemblages featuring a high level of formal complexity that nonetheless fits programmatic and ergonomic requisites.

Synthesis of contemporary CAD techniques and CAD/CAM technologies can be seen in a variety of the Unit 20 projects, as demonstrated by Tobias Klein's Synthetic Syncretism project.[4] More than dexterous modelling and rendering skills, such work relies on being performed with surgical precision without, however, abandoning the creative (formal) richness of his poetic thinking: the process requires the 3-D scanning of existing bone formations around which a series of lavishly designed digital 'plasms' are ergonomically developed.

Kenny Tsui (Unit 20), Voided Veilism, Rome, 2005–07
The project entails a chapel extension at the Basilica of San Clemente, itself a complex of three churches built one above the other. Apart from the intricacy of post-parametric geometries, various architectural references re-enact a challenging conversation on sacred spaces, religious decorative patterns and figural ornaments. These are constructed within the various historic sediments of the basilica in which mesh skins become fleshscapes that exfoliate, breathe, sweat and bleed, feeding the appetite for miracles, prophecies and apparitions.

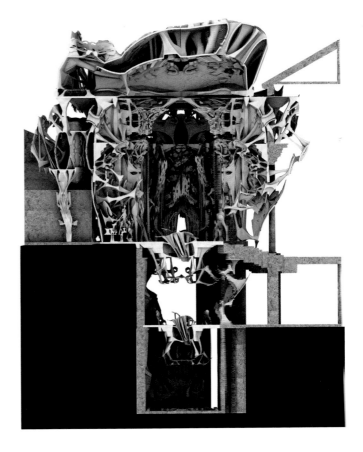

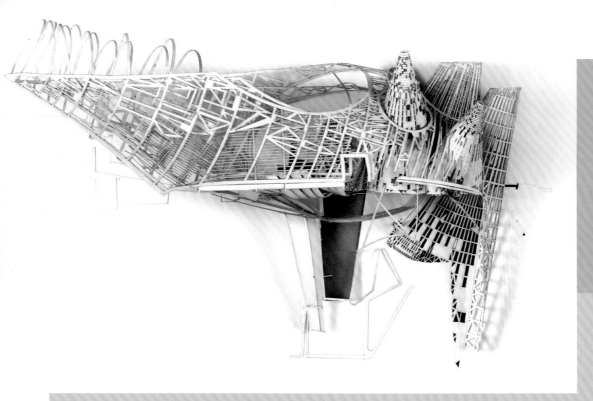

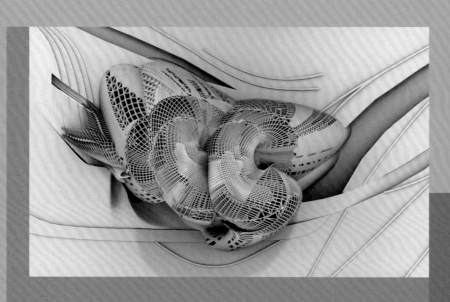

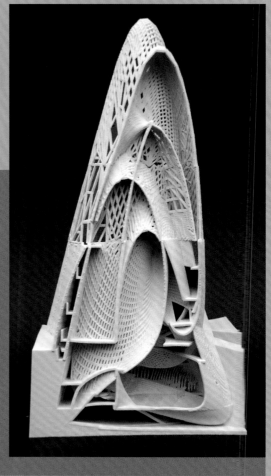

Jay Williams (Unit 20), Convoluted Tectonics, Rome, 2006–07
The project proposes a new pilgrimage chapel in the Domitilla catacombs on the outskirts of Rome. Various ritualistic routes for pilgrims along with paths for tourists interlock and spiral downwards, creating a new access to the catacombs. Intersecting walls, ramps and domes form open spaces of celebration with hidden pockets that embed confessionals, chapels and altars, as well as services for the arriving pilgrims.

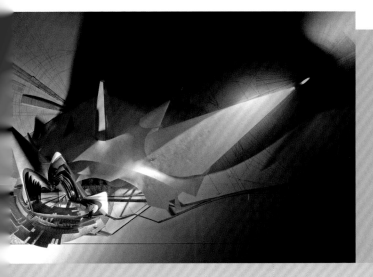

Sara Shafiei (Unit 20), Anamorphic Tectonics, Rome, 2006–07
The design of a theatre for magicians readdresses the sensuality, the 3-D depth and ornamental richness of the Italian baroque. Notions of magical illusion and geometric anamorphosis generate surgically constructed laser-cut models that describe the functional solution of the circulation, as well as the spatial complexity of this realm of projections, performances and illusions.

A different expression of an intuitive, non-linear yet synthetic approach can be observed in the work of Kenny Tsui, which explores the ornamental density of an inhabitable architectural flesh. The sumptuousness of his formal language and creation of sublime interiors are the result of a reinterpretation of premodern typologies and narratives of spiritual spaces.

Tectonic and ornamental, as well as structural and stylistic synthesis, is further achieved in the extraordinary models handcrafted by Sara Shafiei. Informed by studies of magic and illusion, her analogue assemblages of digitally modelled laser-cut cone surfaces are magnificently choreographed, unravelling exuberant yet functional spatial arrangements. Ultimately, architecture prompts a new relationship between spectator (body) and spectacle (architecture).

Other explorations of Convoluted Flesh can also be observed in Jay Williams' maquettes. In his Convoluted Tectonics, an array of complex 3-D circulation systems is convoluted within the substance of architecture, creating mysterious and emotionally loaded atmospheric inner spaces.

In the end, in all the examples mentioned, the concept of Convoluted Flesh readdresses the relationships of facade (expression, reception, materiality) and interior (effect, action, space), of fixedness (stasis, corporeality of matter) and festiveness (movement, celebration of space), of below (matter, function) and above (manner, vision), of being (manifestation) and bogus (magic), of body and architecture. It sees a great potential in sublime, blissful and mysterious conditions as potentially opening up new aesthetic, spatial or material possibilities that are not as limited as its technologically driven and form-generating counterparts. Above all, it allows the creation of visions in which the depth of the architectural flesh is, more than anything, convoluted, poetic and synthetic. △

Notes
1. We are here contrapointing, for example, Ali Rahim and Hina Jamelle's definition of 'elegance' and its seminal role in contemporary architectural design. We believe that sophistication in architecture is not the exclusive result of a high mastery of scripting techniques and aesthetic elegance, but rather of a careful consideration of a variety of values, including structural, spatial and social, along with technical expertise and poetics. This approach goes beyond the significance of 'visual intelligence', 'presence, formal balance, refinement of features and surface, and restrained opulence' that both argue for. See Ali Rahim and Hina Jamelle, 'Elegance in the age of digital technique', in *Architectural Design: Elegance*, Vol 77, No1, Wiley-Academy, 2007, pp 6, 9.
2. This is a metaphoric understanding of the architectural flesh. There are other interpretations of flesh, including human, aesthetic, digital and biological flesh (or better, neo-biological flesh), the latter being the focus of the forthcoming issue of *Architectural Design: Neoplasmatic Design*, guest-edited by Marcos Cruz and Steve Pike (Nov/Dec 2008).
3. Techniques are here understood as process and method, technics as skills and functions, and technologies as scientific knowledge and applications.
4. This particular project by Tobias Klein was supervised in 2005/06 by Marjan Colletti and Shaun Murray.

The Memory of an Elephant

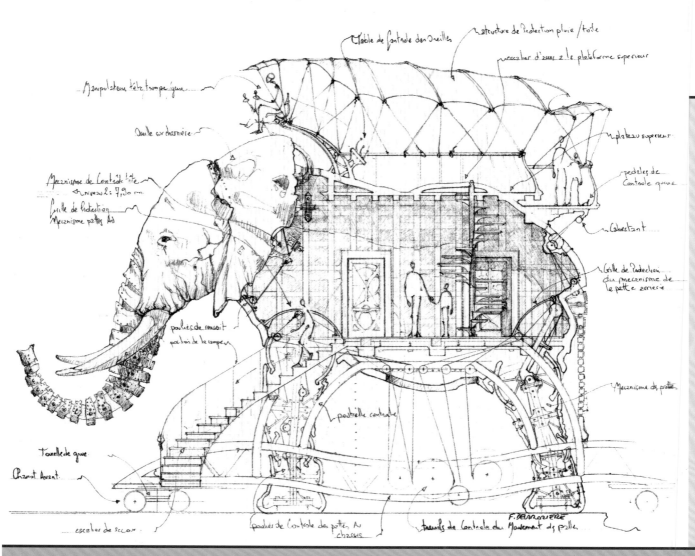

Structure de Protection pluie / toile

Table de Contrôle des Oreilles

escalier d'accès 2 la plateforme supérieur

Manipulateur tête trompe yeux

plateau supérieur

Oreille sur charnière

pedales de Contrôle queue

Mecanisme de Contrôle tête
niveau 2: 7,90 m

Cabestant

Grille de Protection
Mecanisme patte Av

Grille de Protection
du mecanisme de
la patte arrière

poulies de renvoi
position de la rampe

Mecanisme de patte

poutrelle centrale

Tourelle de queue

Chariot Avant

F. DELAROZIERE

escalier de secour

poulies de Contrôle des pattes Av
chassis

treuils de Contrôle du Mouvement des patte

La Machine, The Grand Elephant, Nantes, France, 2007
Section through the Grand Elephant, a new sibling to the
Sultan's Elephant that travelled to London in 2006 (graphite
on paper). 'Drawing a large elephant, which is capable of
transporting 30 people, on paper became a fragile moment
uniting compositional elements with a hierarchy of the
senses. It is in this way that a technical drawing in pencil
comes into being,' says François Delarozière.

A mechanical, 'magical menagerie' is emerging out of the disused shipyard of Nantes in western France. For **Bob Sheil** the project was first embodied by the spectacle of a giant elephant being paraded through the streets of central London in 2006. He describes how the collective of designers at La Machine are creating creatures through carefully contrived production and performance routines.

La Machine, The Sultan's Elephant, Regent Street, London, 2006
François Delarozière, co-director of La Machine, conducts the manipulators as they guide the Sultan's Elephant along Regent Street.

The French city of Nantes has long navigated the hazy line between the exotically imaginative and the fantastically real. The birthplace of sci-fi pioneer Jules G Verne, it also has an important place in France's history as a primary port and a centre for innovative shipbuilding and submarine construction. At the city's centre is the Île de Nantes, a tapering landform that divides the Loire for 5 kilometres (3.1 miles). The island's decline in the late 20th century, and subsequent passage through competing visions for commercial regeneration, maps the city's quest to rekindle its imaginative tradition. This spirit is most evident in the ribs of the former Dubigeon shipyards, an assemblage of post-industrial wreckage reskinned in the summer of 2007 to shelter the extraordinary goings on of La Machine, a collective of designers, makers, engineers, choreographers and theatrical performers led jointly by Pierre Oréfice and François Delarozière.

In their own words, La Machine is an urban project whose aim for Nantes is to conceive of a different city: a city of movement, and a city of the imagination. How this will be manifest will be appreciated by those who have witnessed any of La Machine's extraordinary city spectacles, such as the Sultan's Elephant tour of central London in May 2006, a collaborative event with theatre group Royale de Luxe. The Sultan's Elephant, a 15-metre (49.2-foot) high, 43-ton wheezing mechanical mammal, was coaxed along by 18 costume-clad performers and a hoard of spellbound followers over the course of its two-day 'surprise' visit. The event was only made known to the public by the unexplained appearance of a wooden rocket half buried in a crater of asphalt, clay and steam early in the morning on the first day of the event at Waterloo Place.

London's renowned ambivalence to the unexpected and spectacular was tested as a vast crowd converged in search of the improbable. For François Delarozière, public and civic engagement is critical to understanding La Machine's work as architecture: 'One speaks of architecture in this sense as a living body, in other words a system, not just an object. The elephant is a machine that reveals its skeleton as a steel frame, its muscles as pistons, its veins as hydraulics and its heart as a motor, but, more importantly, it is constructed and assembled as a deliberate evocation of something other than the image of the object, something that is brought to life by action and reaction. An architecture of movement.'

Despite the exquisite fluency and detail of his hand drawings, which he refers to as 'instructions to make', and his academic background in anatomy, Delarozière is not particularly interested in the elephant looking like an elephant, nor is other creations, such as the ray fish or shrimp, closely resembling nature. The purpose of the works, he says, is their transgression of the real and the imaginary. They are made to partially resemble creatures which, through their illusiveness in the real world and proliferation in the narrative world, have entered into myth. It is the capacity of La Machine's creations to project acts of human curiosity, intention, emotion and invention that defines them and gives them their sense of delight. The effort

La Machine, The Grand
Elephant, Nantes,
France, 2007
Carcass study of the Grand
Elephant on display at the
La Machine workshops in
The Île de Nantes, France.

required in translating the machines' behaviour is thus regarded as the primary performance; although assembled to the scale of medium-size buildings, these machines are merely props upon which to project imaginary journeys as they undertake voyages through seemingly familiar places.

La Machine's den at the Dubigeon shipyards does not adhere to the traditional secrecy of theatrical superstition. Where once vast submarines slid into the grey-blue of the salty Loire, drawings, models, tools, materials, prototypes and completed machines are all exposed in seamless acts of creation and performance. At first glance, gallery ushers, dressed in gauntlets, spats and boiler suits, appear a dramatic step too far; later, though, the same individuals can be seen in action within a welding booth, by the chop saw, all from the public viewing gallery designed by Patrick Bouchain. Stacks of raw material, rolls of shop drawings, arrays of jigs, and disparate fabricating processes are clearly visible as inseparable acts of the ongoing spectacle. Delarozière compares this transparency to the strings that connect the marionette with its manipulator. It is the evidence rather than the erasure of human involvement that prompts imagination. What might be thought of as 'human error' is a deliberate attempt to convey the translation of

ideas from image to artefact as a physiological human endeavour. For him the key component is that the audience reads human intention, and the effort required to translate it, as the primary performance.

This is all quite apparent in the carefully choreographed script that stretches from sketch to promenade. The fine line between hands-on and computational methodology, however, lies not far beneath the spectacle of La Machine's production and performance routines. Exquisite as they are, Delarozière's drawings do not encapsulate all the information required to fabricate, test, assemble or engineer these works, nor do they rely on the embellishment of workshop conversation for completion. They certainly inspire confidence, a not unimportant role for a design whose primary purpose is to result in the manufacture of a complex artefact. They certainly allude to the artefact's quality, scale, position of structure, scope of articulation and so on. They certainly occupy a dominant place in the initiation, portrayal and placement of imagination as

From analogue to digital, from static to dynamic, and from live to recorded performance. The design, fabrication, assembly and performance study of the elephant's trunk is previewed through digital simulation, tested in fabrication, and both physically and digitally manipulated in performance

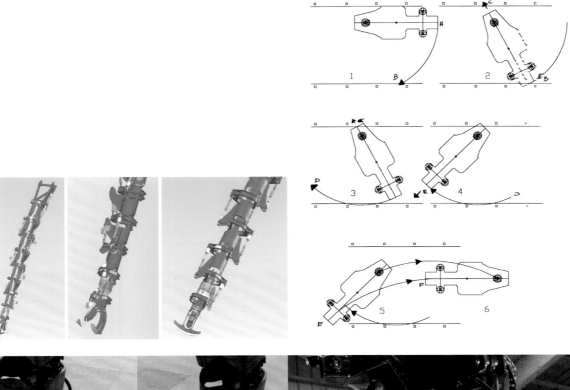

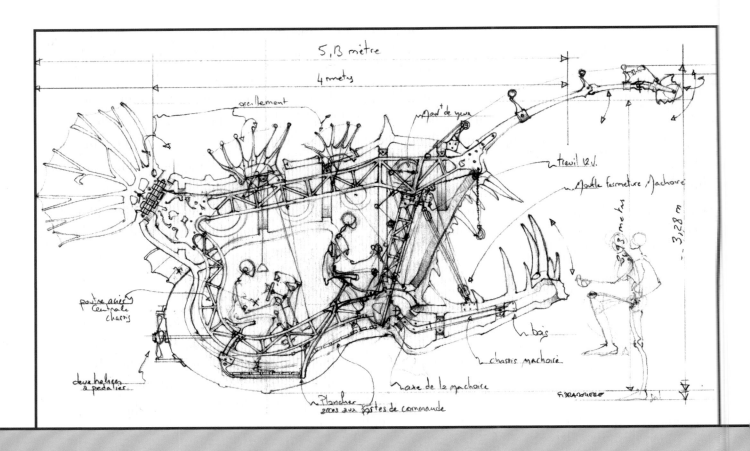

La Machine, La Luminaire des Grands Fonds (The Deep-Sea Angler Fish), Île de Nantes, France, 2007
Sectional study for La Luminaire des Grands Fonds, one of many extraordinary machines under construction for Le Mondes sous Marin (The World below Water), prototypes for an ongoing proposal for a vast carousel in Nantes of imaginary deep-sea creatures. François Delarozière describes his drawings as his language, his way of telling stories: 'It is the starting point of either the studies or the construction. Most of the time the object diverts from the drawing, but I do not modify the sketch which exists independently. They have their own life as drawings.'

La Machine, Le Poission Pirate (The Pirate Fish), Île de Nantes, France, 2007
Le Poisson Pirate located in La Machine's exhibition space while it awaits the future construction of Le Mondes sous Marin.

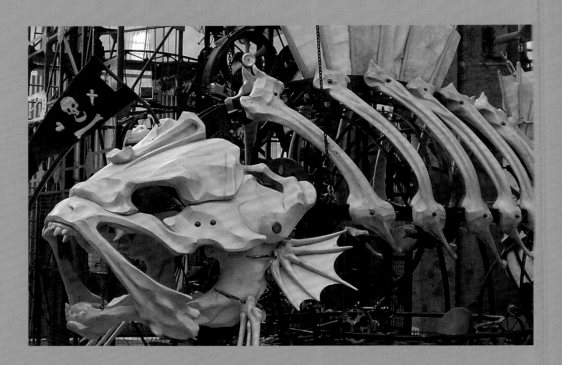

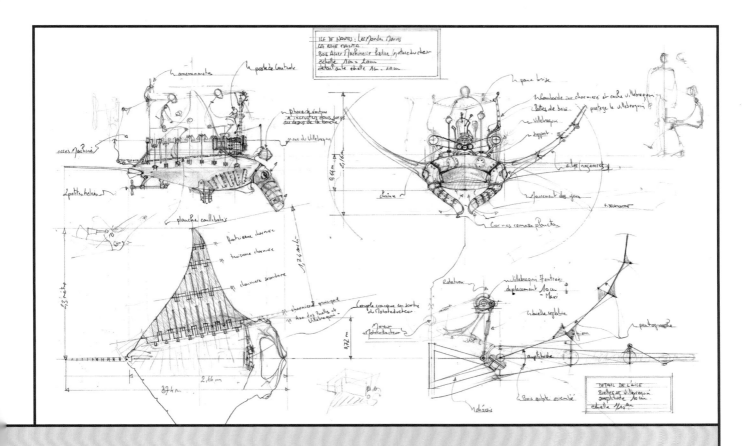

La Machine, La Raie Manta (The Manta Ray), Île de Nantes, France, 2007
Preliminary fabrication studies for La Raie Manta. Delarozière's drawings seem to capture all that is necessary to evoke the idea and the information on how to make it. Although followed by extensive embellishment in digital and analogue media, it is remarkable how often the final outcome resembles the detail of early studies.

the central role of La Machine's activities. But for conversion to the real thing they pass through a number of digital formats and processes, including 3-D scanning, modelling, animation and fabrication. Occupying a clear place in the gallery, the display of how digital technologies are deployed in the fabrication process is not concealed. However, the presentation conveys them as merely practical and efficient tools rather than a means to challenge or evolve design. The sketch remains the blueprint.

Far more curious is the deployment of processing technologies in the performance of the machines. On big occasions their performance is always live. Transmission of human intention and interaction from conductor to marionette, from mechanical nervous system to articulated limbs, from induced movement to the illusion of behaviour, and finally to the mind of the audience, is magical. What is less apparent is that while this is going on, the performance is recorded as a digital script. Past performances can therefore be recalled at any time later, to review the most or least successful movements or responses. While, again, digital technologies are deployed for purposes of practicality and efficiency, their presence provokes a fascinating line of questioning on what might be possible if they were accepted as a system integral to the performance. Could the machines learn to read the city as they march through it? Could they teach us a thing or two about the way that we use it? Could they generate indigenous offspring? La Machine's projects are not architecture in the conventional sense, but they present an extraordinary mirror to it. Thus they should not be dismissed as mere street theatre, albeit on a spectacular scale. Within the mechanical menagerie is a deep well of magical inspiration. ᴆ

Thinking

with Matter

Mark West considers the qualities of the analogue against the digital in the context of his work at the Centre for Architectural Structures and Technology (CAST) at Manitoba. Unable to fault the computer's ability to provide complex calculations for the fabrication of forms, he insists that the fidelity and investigative potential that he has found in the reality of the physical model and hand-drafted drawing have yet to be surpassed.

Plaster test model for sprayed-concrete thin-shell panel, 2007
Detail of a spray-plaster, thin-shell analogue model used to develop the 2.4-metre (7.9-foot) tall thin-shell wall panel. This photograph shows a small portion of a 65-centimetre (25.6-inch)

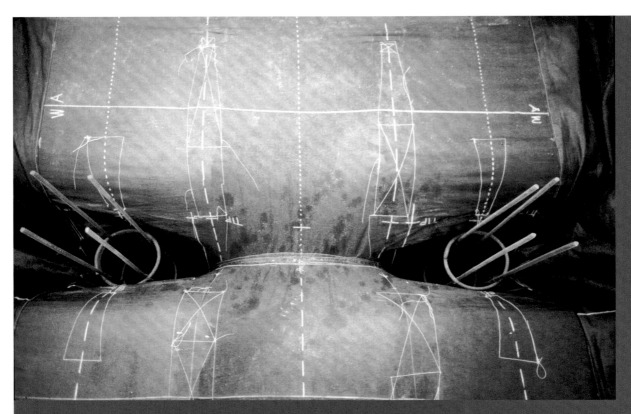

Slab to column form detail, 1992
A view looking down on an early experimental formwork design for a
cast-in-place, one-way structural slab. Two flat sheets of geotextile
fabric, supported from below on shoring beams, are joined to each
other to produce a mould to form a pair of columns, a transverse 'beam
drop' and a ribbed slab. Only the column reinforcing is shown here.

Research at the Centre for Architectural Structures and
Technology (CAST) at the University of Manitoba in
Canada is grounded in physical analogues. CAST
researchers think through drawings made of powder
(graphite, chalk) and physical models contrived to
function as much like their full-scale counterparts as
possible. 'Model' is always both noun and verb.

The constructions produced are essentially 'method
prototypes' rather than miniature objects (though they
serve this function as well), and these analogue
models have proven themselves to be very reliable.
Over 18 years of research it has been found that if
something is buildable in CAST's analogue models, it
will be buildable at full scale. The fidelity of the
models is due to the analogous nature of the materials
used (plaster to model concrete, light fabrics to model
industrial geotextiles, and so on), and to the fact that
tension forces scale linearly, making mechanical
comparisons directly proportional for the most part,
and highly intuitive.

Historical precedents for this way of working include, for example,
Gaudí's hanging model of the Colonia Güell Chapel near Barcelona,
the soap films of Frei Otto, and the hanging fabric shell models of
Heinz Isler. In each case their forms were generated in the realm of
linear tension, allowing complex full-scale geometries and
constructions to be modelled and developed without the need for
computers. Now, of course, we have access to computer-modelling
software, which was unavailable to the early great explorers in this
realm. We are faced with a conscious choice to think and work
through physical analogues.

A physical model (as verb) is excellent because, bound as it is in
actual reality (AR), it is qualitatively rich: full of dense information
about physical forces and strains, construction sequence and detail.
It is very difficult, however, to get quantitative information out of this
kind of model.[1] Digital models, on the other hand, are excellent
because they are rich in quantity: indeed, they are composed of
quantities, and this content makes them invaluable in any building
culture that must calculate before constructing. Calculations for
structures composed of planar surfaces and uniform section volumes
are simple enough to be carried out manually. Structures composed

Beam model formwork, 2003
A 1.5-metre (4.9-foot) model formwork used to work out the construction method for a 12-metre (39.4-foot). reinforced-concrete beam with double cantilevers. This mould, made from a light 'rip-stop' nylon fabric, was filled with plaster. Both the model and the full-scale reinforced-concrete beam are formed in a single flat sheet of fabric stretched into the gap between two plywood 'tables'.

Full-scale fabric formwork beam cast, 2003
Full-scale, 12-metre (39.4-foot) fabric beam formwork filled with concrete. This is the full-scale equivalent of the 1.5-metre (4.9-foot) analogue formwork. The black fabric mould is a flat rectangle of inexpensive geotextile fabric.

of complex curves, such as those generated by tension or compression surfaces and flexible moulds, are more difficult to quantify and predict. Behold the sad scene of the architect who cannot calculate what can be built. For this we need digital models. Indeed, CAST is actively searching for partners who can help in digitising the forms it has found physically.

Some digital models are essentially equivalent to their physical counterparts. For example, relatively small milled objects or objects produced from milled moulds can be the end product of a seamless line from digital model to industrial computer numerically controlled (CNC) production. But for larger things cast from assembled moulds (such as buildings), this line is broken by the necessity for handwork. Digitally generated architectural form, rich as it may be in quantity and calculation, remains in this sense disconnected from the world of

Branching column model test, 2007
Close-up detail of a plaster model for a fabric-formed branching column, showing about 6 centimetres (2.4 inches) of a 31- centimetre (12.2-inch) high model used to design the formwork for a 10-metre (32.8-foot) full-scale prototype column.

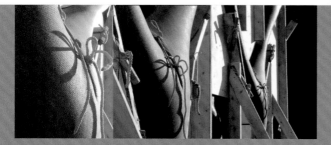

Full-scale branching column formwork, 2007
Composite photograph of branching column formworks filled with concrete. This method uses modified standard plywood wall-formwork, with geotextile fabric form-liners, to cast fabric-formed columns (or, alternatively, concrete walls with fabric-formed pilasters).

12-metre fabric-cast beam, 2003
A 12-metre (39.4-foot) double-cantilever, reinforced-concrete beam cast in a single flat sheet of fabric. A flexible fabric mould vastly simplifies the formation of beams that follow their bending moment curves. This produces beautiful structures that significantly reduce dead weight and materials consumed in construction.

Chalk wall drawings/beam end studies, 2004
The walls of the CAST laboratory are painted with chalkboard paint, giving us large surfaces on which to draw out our ideas. The chalk drawings shown here explore possible constructions and configurations for the ends (support condition) of variable-section, fabric-formed T-beams. Below these drawings is our device for drawing bending moment curves and the placement of reinforcing steel (a hanging string and a simple spline).

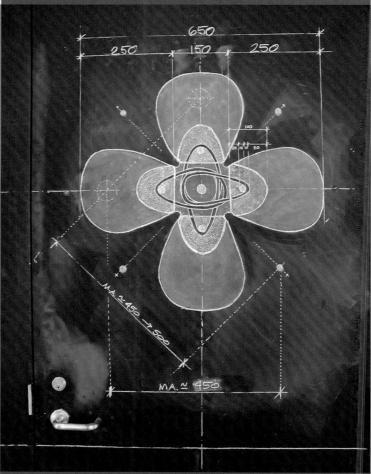

Chalk wall drawing/1:1 column plan detail study, 2003
Full-scale plan-section drawing through a composite (four-part) reinforced-concrete, fabric-formed column design for La Ciudad Abierta (the Open City) in Ritoque, Chile. Full-scale chalk drawings such as this allow us to work out the placement of reinforcing steel final construction dimensions.

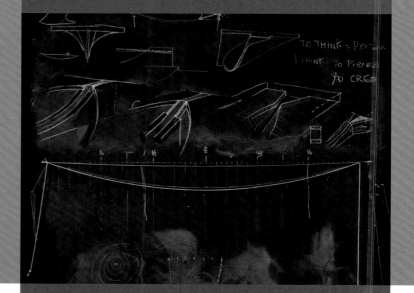

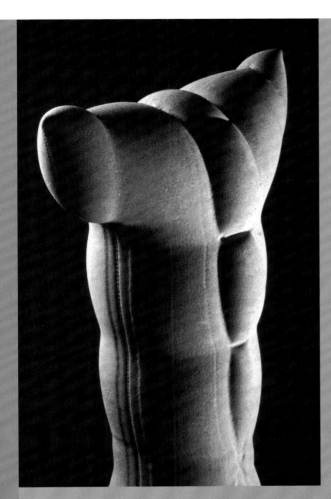

Reinforced–concrete bollard detail, 1995
Like all of CAST's work, this bollard is formed in moulds made from
flat rectangles of fabric: no tailoring for curvatures, just flat sheets
directly off the roll. In this case the mould was a sheet of Lycra
spandex. A stretch-resistant outer jacket was used to partially control
the deflection of the spandex.

physical construction by virtue of its size. By and large,
complex digitally generated forms are extremely
difficult to get out of the computer and into the
physical world. Behold the sorry scene of the architect
with the digitally generated blob begging the builder
and the engineer to figure out how to construct the
marvellous design. Economy usually dictates that these
ambitious designs will tend to devolve towards simpler,
conventional forms. If the money and will exists to
actually build some difficult new form (an investment
in the 'wow effect', perhaps), then here is the sorry
scene of resources and capital squandered in the
difficult task of physically constructing something
whose origin has no physically constructed reference.

Based on these considerations, physical model
prototypes are by far the best way to find and develop
new, buildable architectural forms. The speed and awesome
resolution of AR allows us to think, imagine and discover quickly in
an inexpensive, non-punitive environment. Naturally, the relative
quality and shortcomings of the analogues will determine how far
towards full-scale construction knowledge these models take us.
Nevertheless, their greatest virtue remains that no matter what kind
of form we find, we already know how to build it because the form
was found by building.

Form research at CAST embraces both sculptural and structural
forms. The search for sculptural form does not begin with a design,
but rather with a choice of materials and methods. Here the forms
that are found are given rather than 'designed', as the materials
themselves dictate their final disposition in space through the
urgencies of natural law. The search for structural form, on the other
hand, is more directed in the attempt to follow specific, efficient and
calculable force 'paths' through matter. Although certain aspects of
these structural forms are decided upon by the materials themselves,
the overall structural geometry is known before making begins.

Looking for construction methods to form efficiently shaped
structures is like attempting to hit the centre of a pre-existing target
with a rifle. The search for sculptural form, however, is more like
shooting a shotgun against a wall and drawing bull's-eyes around all
the holes.[2] The 'shotgun' approach is CAST's basic research, to learn
what is possible without preimposing artificial limitations. In this, the
researchers work like artists. The 'rifle' approach is the applied
research where techniques selected from all the interesting shotgun
holes are used to construct some specific instrumental thing.

CAST's research is specifically architectural in that it
simultaneously partakes of the narrow scientific traditions of
engineering and the techniques of open discovery proper to the 'fine'
arts. The evaluation of what is found is determined by its efficiency
(practical, economical, sustainable) and by its beauty (as felt. When
simplicity of construction, economy of material consumption and a
kind of effortless beauty and evocation coincide, we know we are on
the right track. Any ambition towards this kind of simple complexity
requires the assistance of Matter (who always knows best). △

This work is supported by the Social Science and Humanities Research Council of
Canada (SSHRC) and the Lafarge Construction Materials Group, Winnipeg, Canada.
Special thanks to CAST's Team Gravity: graduate research assistants Chris Wiebe, Paul
Christenson, Aynslee Hurdal, Leif Friggstad, Mike Johnson, Kyle Martens and Tom
Alston, and engineer and PhD candidate Fariborz Hashemian.

Notes
1. This difficulty is attested to by the fact that Gaudí only used his hanging maze once,
reverting afterwards to standard graphic statics calculations. Heinz Isler was able to
obtain quantitative information from his physical models only through painstaking and
super-precise handwork, a task so delicate that he refused to let anyone else perform
this work and could not be interrupted without causing disruptions in the consistency of
the data. As described in John Chilton's *Heinz Isler: The Engineer's Contribution to
Contemporary Architecture*, Thomas Telford (London), 2000.
2. I take the 'shotgun' image of research from Steven Vogel's *Life in Moving Fluids: The
Physical Life of Flow*, Princeton University Press (Princeton NJ), 1981, p 3.

Prosthetic Mythologies

The forest wilderness of Kielder in Northumbria is one of England's remotest areas. Sharing an ecology similar to much of northern Scandinavia, Alaska and Canada, it shares none of its native culture or folklore. Only planted in the 1920s, the conifer forests are relatively recent – a graft on the natural landscape. **Kate Davies and Emmanuel Vercruysse** of LIQUID FACTORY describe how their site-specific performance piece sought out the psychological power of the forest, endowing it with 'Prosthetic Mythologies'.

LIQUID FACTORY, Prosthetic Mythologies, Kielder Forest, Northumbria, 2007
Front view of an occupant – a single member of the colony – installed on its tree. The outstretched arms are tensioned to adjacent trees.

The dark interior of a mature section of Kielder Forest.

The sky puts on the darkening blue coat held for it by a row of ancient trees.

Rainer Maria Rilke[1]

In 1926, with British timber stocks depleted by the First World War, the Forestry Commission began planting a new forest at Kielder, Northumbria. Around 150 million non-native conifers were transplanted on to land that had been treeless for centuries. Fifty years later construction began on Kielder Water, the largest manmade reservoir in northern Europe, submerging a number of valley hamlets in the process. At 647 square kilometres (250 square miles), Kielder Forest is the largest in England. Kielder is England's most remote village, boasting the country's darkest skies: a paradoxical landscape at the extremes of both cultivation and wilderness. During a 50-year cycle, the regimented rows of freshly planted saplings evolved into an interior of thick moss and wandering streams. The creaking of trees and heavy mist overlay its depths with mystery and foreboding. The very industry that structures this landscape so pragmatically also enables it to be a wilderness.

Lost Denizens

Kielder shares its ecosystem with vast swathes of Alaska, Siberia, northern Scandinavia and Canada. These ancient boreal or taiga forests exist in a subarctic coniferous band around the globe and are home to a lexicon of mythical denizens that haunt their depths. Much of this forest mythology paints an unsettling picture. In the tribal mythology of North America, the terrifyingly deformed *windigo* inhabits the pine forests of the Northwest Territories. Six metres (20 feet) tall and skeletal, this malevolent spirit is said to eat human flesh with its fanged and lipless mouth, and its hissing breath can be heard for miles around as it travels at great speed through the forest. Much Scandinavian forest mythology talks of beautiful but sinister 'wood-wives' (*skogsrå* or *huldra*) luring travellers into the forest with doleful tunes. Though beautiful face to face, it is said that their backs are hollow and blackened.

Folklore and ritual connect man to his landscape, dancing through the liminal zone between the everyday and the spiritual. Kielder is a forest wilderness devoid of the history of mythology coursing through the ancient boreal zones. It is a prosthetic landscape – a graft – where the connection to the mythological and ceremonial practices of native man has never been established. Mythology can be thought of as a way of expressing

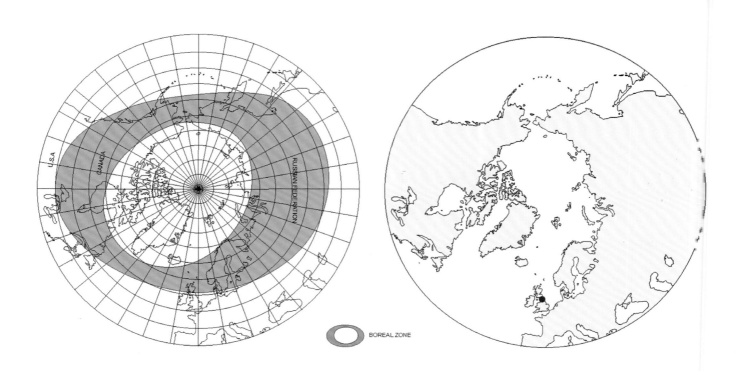

BOREAL ZONE

Diagrams showing the boreal region surrounding the North Pole.

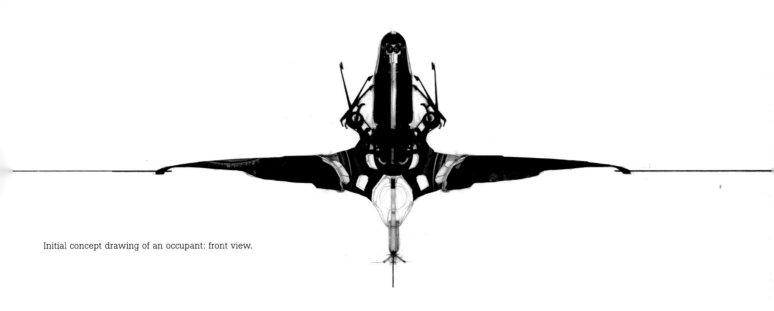

Initial concept drawing of an occupant: front view.

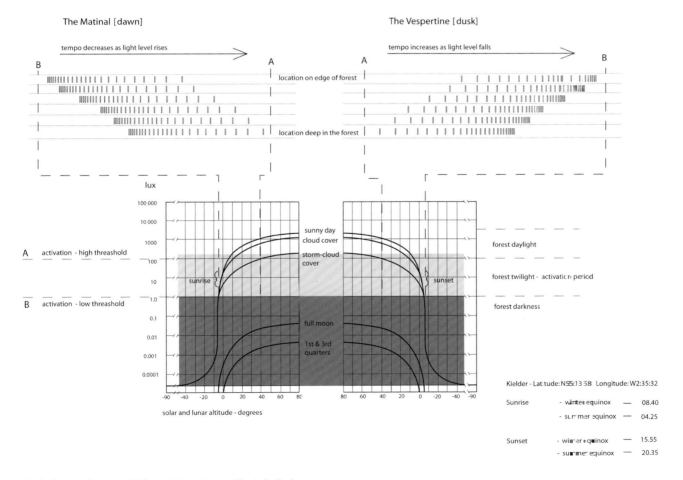

The Matinal [dawn]

tempo decreases as light level rises →

B | A

location on edge of forest

location deep in the forest

The Vespertine [dusk]

tempo increases as light level falls →

A | B

lux

100 000
10 000
1000
100
10
1.0
0.1
0.01
0.001
0.0001

A   activation - high threshold

B   activation - low threshold

sunny day
cloud cover
storm-cloud
cover

sunrise

sunset

full moon

1st & 3rd
quarters

forest daylight

forest twilight - activation period

forest darkness

-90 -40 -20 0 20 40 60 80   80 60 40 20 0 -20 -40 -90

solar and lunar altitude - degrees

Kielder - Latitude: N 55:13 58 Longitude: W 2:35:32

Sunrise   - winter equinox   —   08.40
           - summer equinox   —   04.25

Sunset   - winter equinox   —   15.55
           - summer equinox   —   20.35

Graph showing light thresholds at dusk and dawn. The individual
rhythms produced by the occupants overlap and drop in and out of
phase in response to rising or falling light levels, producing changing
performances dependent on the time of year and weather patterns.

Making one of the master moulds from a section of the wooden form. The aluminium components are then removed from the wooden form and set into the mould to be embedded within the polyurethane during rotational casting.

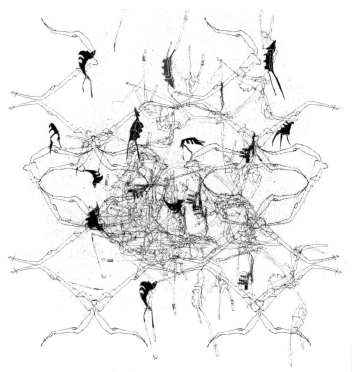

The colony comprises a cluster of autonomous occupants, each reacting independently to its surrounding light condition.

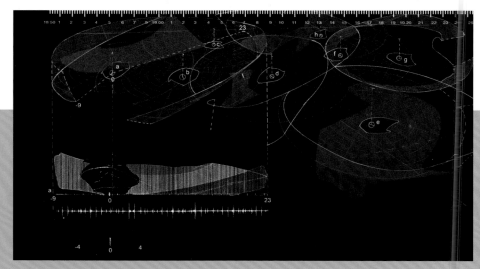

A carved MDF arm. Prototype elements such as this make up the blueprint object.

Each member of the colony expands its territory through sound, creating a dynamic multidirectional soundscape. The drawing shows the occupants' sensory and sonic territories.

Prosthetic Mythologies is an automated performance piece for Kielder Forest in which the forest becomes the stage for a ceremony.

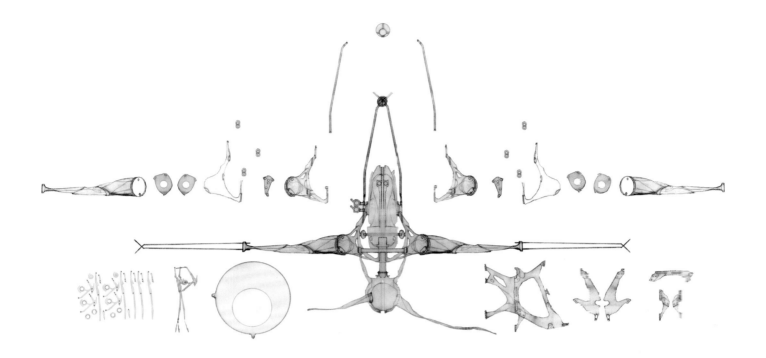

Pattern drawing showing the individual components of the sound mechanism and structural skeleton, as well as CNC-routed aluminium components for embedding in the polyurethane casts. Each component is constructed from a template so that the entire object can be duplicated.

intangible truths, and forest mythology has its roots in a primal response to the immersive environment of the forest. This is not a wilderness of bracing physical exposure like the mountain, but instead a dark internal wilderness of quiet psychological exposure.

A Crepuscular Performance
Prosthetic Mythologies is an automated performance piece for Kielder Forest in which the forest becomes the stage for a ceremony. A colony of sculptural and sonic automata reside within an unspecified plot deep in the forest. They are crepuscular – activated only at low light levels. Their combined response to the specific light conditions of their individual site forms a rhythmic composition in two parts: the Vespertine (dusk) and the Matinal (dawn). The colony expands its territory dynamically through sound. During dusk, at a low light threshold, each individual occupant begins to hammer out its private rhythm, each activating sequentially depending on its location, with those deeper in the forest activating first. The tempo of each rhythm increases as the light falls, and builds to a crescendo of rhythmic layers falling in and out of phase with each other, evoking a feverish ritual. Then, one by one, they fall silent, awaiting dawn.

Twilight in the forest is a traditional setting for mythology and folklore. The French describe twilight as 'Entre chien et le loup' (between dog and wolf), which captures the unsettling transformation that occurs at dusk. As shadows seep into the forest it becomes a threatening place. The project thus draws on the psychological power of the forest, seeking to inhabit the dark evocative interior of Kielder Forest with a prosthetic mythology. ⊿

Note
1. From the poem 'Evening', by Rainer Maria Rilke, in *The Selected Poetry of Rainer Maria Rilke*, ed and trans Stephen Mitchell, Random House (New York), 1982, p 13.

Evan Douglis Studio, Flora_flex, Rotterdam/New York, 2007
Oblique view of the Flora_flex membrane showing the excitability of the surface.

Flora_Flex

In Search of Synthetic Immortality

Evan Douglis performs alchemy, bringing to life from the inaminate 'the natural' with his genetically inspired Flora_flex prefab modular building system. He demonstrates the beauty, intricacy and opulence inherent in pursuing flowering plant morphology as a model for surface variation.

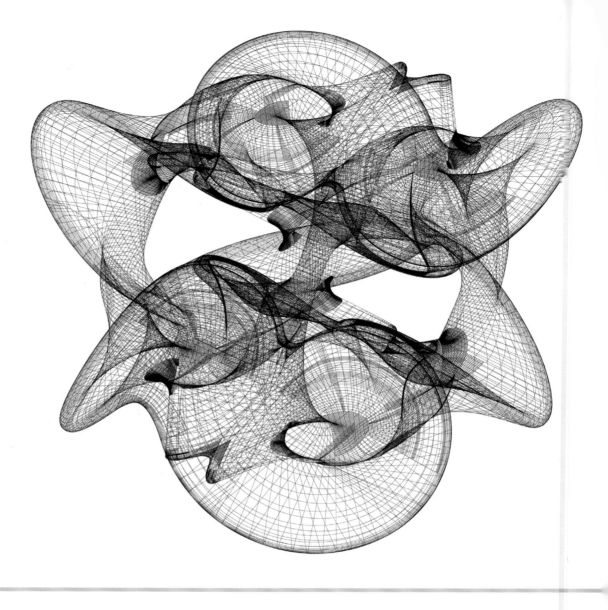

With rising interest in emergent systems as the new organisational model for a planet undergoing constant change, the opportunities to develop a more robust biomimetic approach in architecture are becoming increasingly more attractive. The once exotic and ineffable metamorphosis of the chameleon octopus, the otherworldly bioluminescence of the sea cucumber, the strange gelatinous and reconfigurable anatomy of a comb jelly creature, and the unsettling carnivorous appetite of a Venus flytrap are no longer unobtainable manifestations for the impatient futurist. The dazzling and unique qualities of invertebrates and flora are just a few examples of the complex systems of living organisms now being assessed and decoded as generative computational data deployable in architectural experimentation.

The bridge between organic and inorganic systems as a transfer of essential genetic information is not a new proposition. The legacy of alchemy, in a variety of fields, sought the creation of a parallel animistic universe through the transmutation of matter. Conceived as an extension of our timeless desire to bring inanimate material to life, a quest for synthetic immortality has preoccupied our imagination for centuries.

Evan Douglis Studio, Flora_flex, Rotterdam/New York, 2007

above: Oblique view of wire-frame mesh showing the extensive variety of involuted surfaces intrinsic to the main unit.

opposite: Elevation of wire-frame mesh showing the high degree of surface complexity distributed around the centre toroid ring.

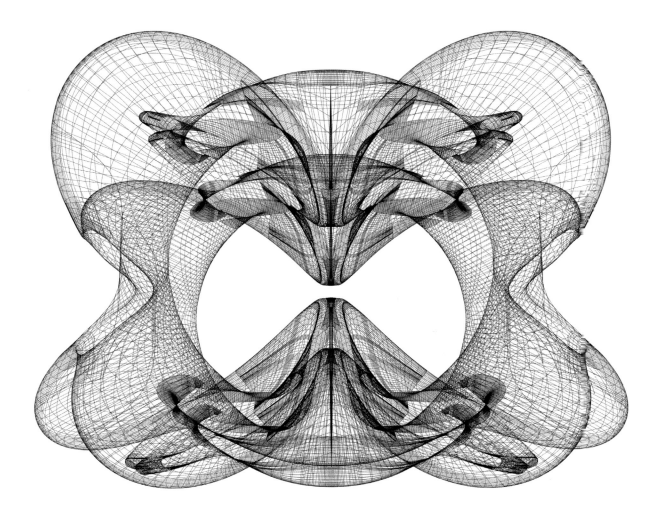

Given the present predisposition within architectural evolution to further understand and control complexity, next-generation animate assemblies will comprise more complex scripted equations capable of re-enacting the most spectacular effects. Harnessing the unlimited power of programming as a vast hereditary engine for emergent design, we will see an unimaginable increase in surface and behavioural variation at a level of intricacy and control unparalleled in the history of digital design.

Flora_flex: A Manifesto

In appreciation of the current shift in architecture towards the 'play of surface', the Flora_flex prefab mocular building system set out to test parametric design as a generative source for producing infinite variation. Combining an interest in botany, skeleton morphology, topology, optical effects and emergent growth patterns, it represents a new era of computationally derived membranes that maximise the use of 'intricacy' as a contemporary design strategy to increase desirability and use.

Currently offered as a prototype screen and assembled as an interchangeable alphabet of load-bearing units, the array of surface relief, changing transparency and recombinatory options now available to the consumer all subscribe to a promising future in an architecture of increased flexibility and control. Slip-cast, injection-moulded or 3-D-printed out of a variety of space-age materials, the Flora_flex prefabricated wall system aims to use the most recent advances in material science to bring architecture to life.

right: Elevation of the Flora_flex modular system providing clear evidence of the computational options available within a field comprising an interchangeable puzzle of biologically conceived building components.

below: Detail of Flora_flex surface highlighting: the overall packing logic regulating the modular field, the range of surface expression offered within the kit of parts, and the array of topological nesting formations that emerge unexpectedly.

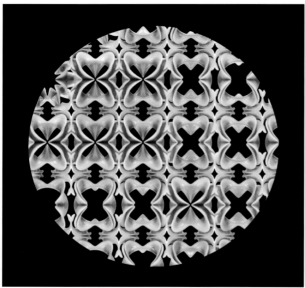

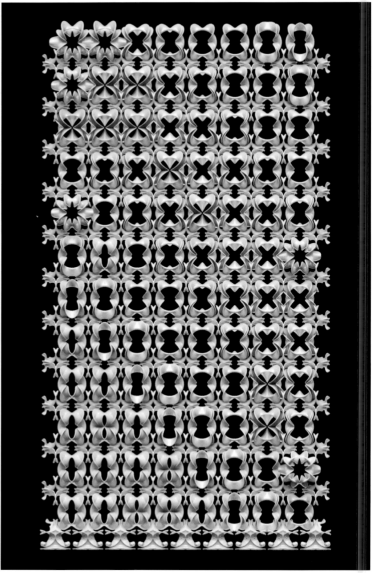

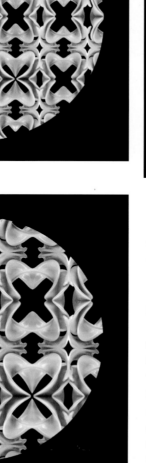

Biomimetic Ornament

In pursuit of a more intelligent, responsive and topologically exuberant architecture, the underlying logic within Evan Douglis Studio's scripted equations continuously looked to nature as a primary source from which to draw inspiration. Flowering plant morphology was targeted as an ideal example of surface variation and retinal effects, and this early precedent model offered essential insight into the complex and mysterious world of a natural time-based system undergoing continuous change. Posited as a complex assembly of delicate radial flange work collectively dilating in relation to a perpetually changing cycle of photosynthesis, transpiration and pollination, the organisational logic of a simple flower is an impressive example of an evolved ecology of interests. As a relational organism that is symbiotically dependent on its environmental context and surrounding species for its survival, it personifies the larger promise of an emergent system as a blend of recurring patterns favouring difference and similarity.

Beginning with the primary (o) unit of construction, the priority from the start for the Flora_flex system was to develop a repetitive module that maximised the illusory properties of a surface appearing to undergo continuous distortion or flux in relation to a changing picture plane. Analogous to a primitive ambient isotopic surface found in the world of topology, the helical rotation of the projected flanges spinning around the centre torus ring served to produce a similar ocular vibration, necessary to generate the appearance of an anamorphic surface.

As is typical in any modular system, there is always the critical reciprocity between the unit and the field. The unique challenge is to sustain variation at all costs in favour of creating an excitable kaleidoscope of effects that operate at varying scales and perspectival positions. In response, while the base geometry of the main unit remained fixed in terms of the constancy of the torus, the extensive development of the scripted flange choreographies offered the wide range of combinatory options necessary to produce the intended complexity and difference required to create an emergent skin.

In conjunction with the main units that regulate the overall transparency and surface expression across the membrane, a complementary (+) module was also developed. As a critical structural and topological accessory, the (+) unit fulfils a series of design priorities essential to the overall performance of the Flora_flex system. Acting as an intermediary building component as it transfers loads diagonally across the membrane, this secondary module serves an invaluable role as it brings spatial and structural continuity to an expansive assembly made up of discrete parts. Also offered as a deviant sibling, the (+) unit undergoes a morphological transformation at the ground plane to allow for the necessary divergence of horizontal loads.

Bringing attention to the perpetual reconfiguration of the flower petal as a simple reminder of the wonder of metamorphosis and the power of change, the Flora_flex modular system seeks to re-create a similar unexpected sensation of surprise through the use of changing porosity and surface excess. Conceived as both a game of chance and of purposeful intent, the computational arrangement of modular pieces placed across an expanded field constitutes an architecture of infinite play.

Evolutionary Changes: Future Perfect
Offered as a work in progress, the Flora_flex version here represents the first evolutionary stage of development. In the spirit of any emergent system capable of becoming increasingly more intelligent from one moment to the next, the next generation of scripting

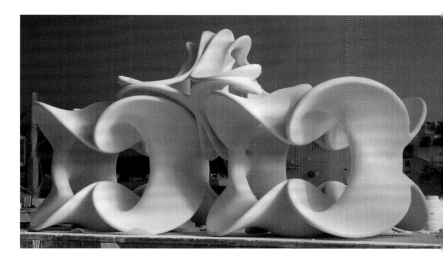

View of the slip-cast ceramic fired prototypes showing a greenware body with a porcelain outer-shell coat.

Oblique view of the polymer-cast prototype building components with a high-gloss urethane paint finish.

Elevation of the Flora_flex
modular system deploying
the single-flange type
repetitively throughout the
entire freestanding wall

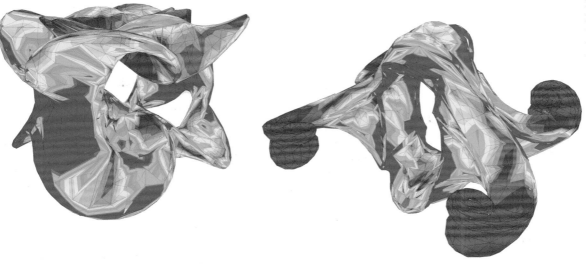

Finite analysis of the
primary building
components highlighting the
greatest amount of
compression stresses in blue.

within the system, capable of offering even greater flexibility, is currently being explored.

In favour of introducing a more advanced modular version, Evan Douglis Studio is currently working to: increase the complexity of the torus beyond the simple doughnut by introducing a variety of knot topologies; generate an ever-expanding menu of flange types that offer an even greater degree of surface variation; develop the morphology of the intermediary units to assume an ever-increasing structural role throughout the field; integrate smart materials within the design and manufacturing process as a means to increase the overall performative value and effects of the system; and to introduce two-way curvature across the membrane in

...THE STUDIO DEVELOPED A SERIES OF SLIP-CAST MOULDS REQUIRED TO MATERIALISE THE PARAMETRIC DESIGN AS CERAMIC MODULAR COMPONENTS.

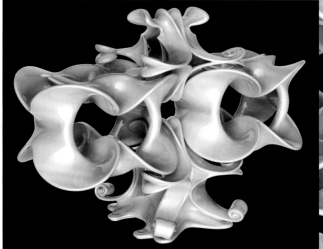

Isolation of the primary building components underlying the Flora_flex modular system. Note the careful attention paid to the articulated interface between the pieces.

Oblique view of the vertical surface showing seemingly animate flanges dilating around the centre void.

pursuit of generating a series of topological bladders en route to the first Flora_flex house.

Manufactured Nature: A Brief History of Production
Given the variety of material and fabrication options available for the production of the first Flora_flex prototype models, it was decided to work with more familiar materials at the start, and over time introduce more sophisticated technologies deemed appropriate to the project. With the generous support of the European Ceramic WorkCentre (EKWC) in the Netherlands in 2007, the studio developed a series of slip-cast moulds required to materialise the parametric design as ceramic modular components. After an extensive trial-and-error period, a set of workable moulds that enabled the casting and firing of full-scale greenware and porcelain pieces was successfully fabricated. A selection of prototype models was presented at the 2007 Rotterdam Biennale.

Subsequent to this work, the Evan Douglis Studio pursued a contemporary material that would be more receptive to mass production and a broad range of building applications. Seeking to utilise a more durable and lightweight material, liquid polymer was selected as an alternative casting material for the next series of Flora_flex prototypes, and an extended set of single-flange components was produced using this fabrication process.

In response to the wider aim of a more responsive and environmentally interactive set of building components, Evan Douglis Studio is currently seeking to incorporate smart materials within its future manufacturing process. Intrigued by the unlimited possibilities for architecture with this new generation of animate materials such as shape memory alloys, pH-sensitive polymers and chromogenic materials, it appears that its most extreme work concerning the Flora_flex project is yet to come. ∆

screens

The screen is a recurring element in the work of Niall McLaughlin Architects. Environmental considerations have provided the opportunity for inclusion of the screen in built works, but it has been embraced by them for its geometric and material qualities, as well as the play it affords with light. The practice has relished the transformative powers of inserting everyday found objects into the screens to provide an additional level of surprise and delight.

This picture-essay illustrates 10 screens designed by Niall McLaughlin Architects over a period of almost 20 years. Looking back over the work, it is interesting to assemble the projects in a way that shows a consistent concern with particular themes relating to arrays, repetition and light. It is not the intention here to make any forced connections in order to underline consistency. However, looking at the collection of images, a number of themes emerge.

The practice enjoys the strategy of making geometric arrays of found materials and objects. The more commonplace the material, the more enjoyable the effect of the resulting transformation. In the projects here, one finds umbrellas, Daz, gold, Cosy Cloches, web-cam footage, disco film, hanging chads, plastic tubes and guttering. Every project also delights in the transformative power of light. Screens have a particular way of manifesting light, holding it within them to create a three-dimensional epiphany. A good screen has a slight fizz to it. Where daylight is used, the screen becomes a timepiece, marking the passage of the sun by transforming the shadows and reflections within its own lattice.

In addition, the use of arrays and the tactic of serial repetition within a laconic geometric order raise certain comparisons with music: the acoustic equivalent of the screens might be a static polyphonic chant. Screens are also paradoxical: they present themselves as two-dimensional, but their essence is three-dimensional. The primary visual buzz occurs as a result of a flipping of perception between 2-D and 3-D.

Certain factors have driven the prevalence of screens in recent architectural production. The consequences of the energy crises on building techniques require laminated, discontinuous construction, forcing architects to consider the separate identities of inner and outer parts of the building envelope. The development of the computer screen as a primary interface between the individual and the wider world promotes this charged layer to special prominence. The Postmodern desire for buildings to manifest themselves as presence, rather than logical order, is therefore pushing architects to seek more direct effects.

Hanging Chads, Private house, London, 2000

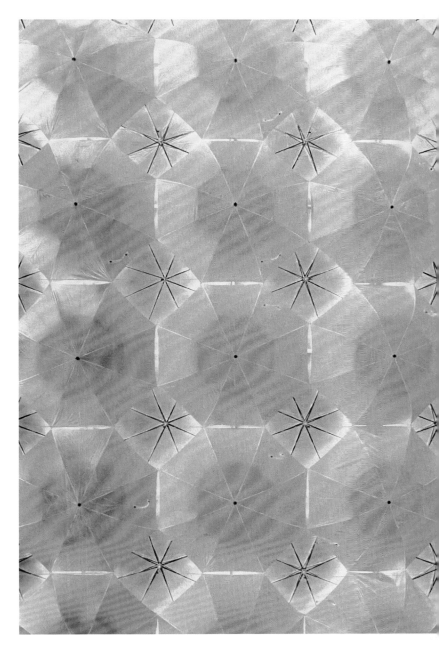

Storm Wall, Bartlett School of Architecture, UCL, London, 1991
Designed and built with Phil Tabor and the students of Unit 17 at the Bartlett School of Architecture, UCL, this geometric array of back-to back umbrellas was intended as a temporary partition in a large hall. The umbrellas were sewn together at their extremities. Two layers of connected umbrellas were placed facing away from each other, half a grid out of sequence, so that the pole of one passed through the centre of the gap between the canopies on the opposite layer. This created a regular, undulating screen with a visible internal latticework. When the screen was demounted, and the umbrellas collapsed, it was carried away in a shopping bag.

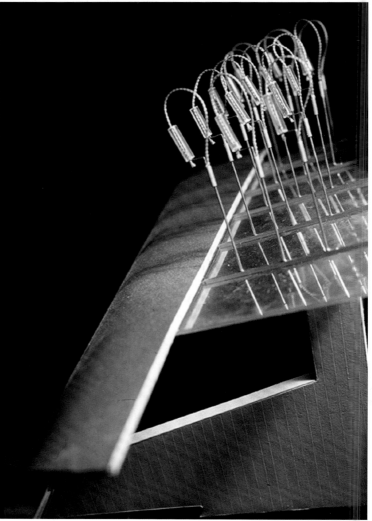

Bloom, RIBA, London, 1996

This strongly scented and illuminated field was designed, in collaboration with artist Martin Richman, as a transformation of the first-floor gallery of the Royal Institute of British Architects (RIBA) on Portland Place. A bed of Daz detergent was laid upon the floor. Two hundred opalescent, house-shaped structures called Cosy Cloches, purchased by mail order from a garden supply company, were arrayed in a regular pattern on the washing powder. Each was lit internally with a UV light, which is invisible by day and blindingly bright after dark. In daylight, the piece was calm and white with naturally repeating shadows falling between the plastic gables. By night, the UV caused the Daz to phosphoresce, electrifying the space between the cloches. Giant mirrors on the ceiling reflected the illuminated rectangle, making it visible to passers-by on the street below, and the detergent perfumed the building for weeks.

Phototropic, Flower Farm, Kettering, Northamptonshire, 1997

This unbuilt project is a pollen laboratory for a flower farm. The south-facing wall is a dense array of solar panels, the energy from which is directed to the north wall where chilling rods cause the cast-glass screen to mist over. The hotter the day, the cooler the wall will become, as it uses all the sun's energy for chilling. The opalescent cool wall is used as a screen for projected real-time images of blooms from the growth-forcing poly tunnels. The project captures the unreal, half-nature–half-machine environment of flower farming, an industry where the rhythms of nature are harnessed to the market using telecommunications.

Hanging Chads, Private house, London, 2000

Here, a two-storey-high tapestry of A4 sheets is held on delicate suspended cables, and screens light from the south entering an ugly old bay window. The sheets are made of silver nickel, which has a silvery, brassy lustre. Each is computer cut with hundreds of triangular leaves, which are pressed by hand so that they stand out from the back in regular repeated folds to create 'hanging chads' (after the scandal in Florida during the US presidential election). The sheets are laid out so that they overlap in the horizontal and vertical plane. Backlight bounces between the layers creating complex effects. Peter Mueller, the project architect, pressed each of the 50,000 triangular leaves using his index finger. However, once completed it was decided that they were set at the wrong angle, so he had to start all over again.

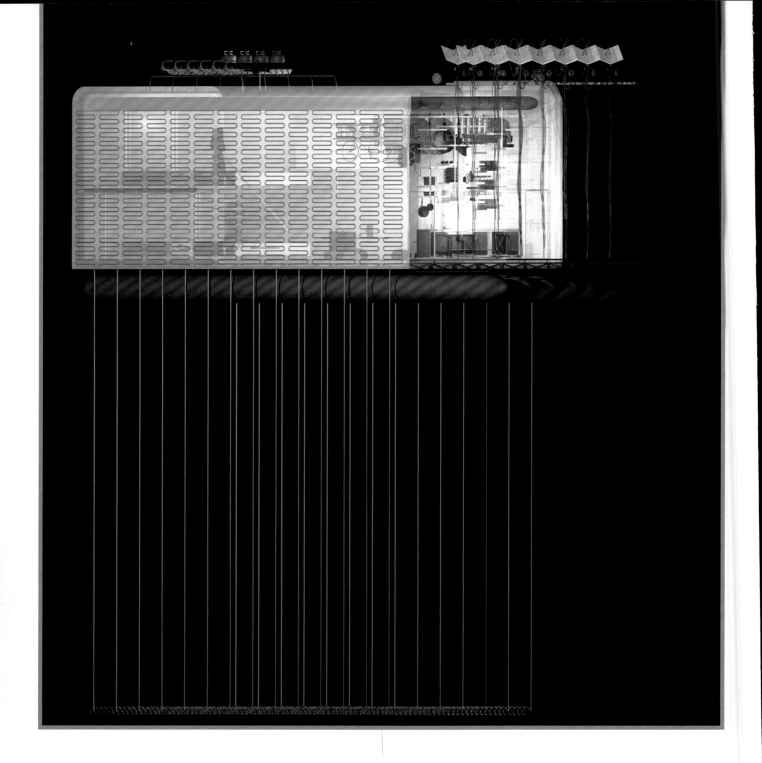

Thermocline, Houseboat, London, 2001

This project was developed for fun in the office, but was later entered in the House of the Future competition, which it won. Since then, the office has received calls from eccentrics around the world promising to build it on a canal in their home town. The external wall is made of layers of fibreglass, glass fibre and thin woven veneer. It is envisaged as a semitranslucent insulated basket. An underfloor heating system, made of regular loops of clear plastic tube carrying water, is arranged in a vertical matrix on the wall and held in place by aluminium heat-transfer plates. This is a proprietary, concealed floor product used vertically, and visibly, in a wall. Water travels through the tubes, pushed by solar-powered pumps, and descends into copper coils hanging in the water below the thermocline. Beneath this layer, the water is at a constant temperature throughout the seasons; thus the whole screen acts as a heat dump. When viewed against the light, the lazy rhythm of the veiled, coiling tubes is intended to resemble that of the veins on one's wrist.

Sprite Major, ARC Architecture Centre, Hull, 2003

In this project the practice worked with the local community to build a small architecture centre by a motorway in a derelict area of Hull. The building was made using technology transferred from other local industries in the area including caravan building, ceramics and chemical dyes, and will move to a new site every three years. Hull, once famous for trawler manufacture, fishing and food processing, has turned its back on the sea. The roof of the building is a translucent, insulated plane tilted towards the traffic flowing over the bridge into the city. It is built like an empty advertising hoarding. A web cam, positioned out in the old fishing grounds beyond Spurn Point, transmits images of the surface of the sea on to projectors illuminating the roof. Each night, the day's weather is played back on to the screen's surface. The images are abstract, but they work subliminally, like a heartbeat, bringing the shifting patterns of the old hinterland back into the city. The light from the projectors filters through the roof into the inter or beneath, bringing a wavering, changeable quality to the space.

Loom, Avenham Park Pavilion, Preston, Lancashire, 2005
Preston is one of the wettest towns in England. This made it
particularly suitable for the manufacture of linen, and by the 19th
century it was prospering as a transatlantic cotton trader. Avenham
Park was built beside the River Ribble by workers temporarily out of
work during the American Civil War. The park is entered from an
elevated position, which looks down on meadows sweeping towards
the river below. For the pavilion, the practice proposed a horizontal
canopy, like a spread-out picnic cloth, which is seen from above by
visitors arriving at the park. The screen is a multicoloured woven layer
that covers cafés, music stands, toilets and a little hall. The mature
avenue of trees along the river passes through the weave. This tense
matrix is held in place by stout, braced timber frames, like a loom.
The roof is designed to catch the frequent rain and make a noisy
event of its journey back to the river. There are gutters, basins and
gargoyles woven into the warp and weft of cables, and wind turbines
and solar panels are held in the array. The building comes into itself
during a downpour when the rain animates the upper canopy. From
the café one can watch water sluicing down into the river and
smearing the windows, obliterating the view.

Iridescence, Peabody Trust Low-cost Housing, Silvertown, Newham, London, 2002

Silvertown once manufactured luxury goods and TNT explosive. Now that it has lost all its factories it has become an eerie post-industrial landscape of Ibis hotels, exhibition halls and Noddy houses. The practice worked with the artist Martin Richman on this low-cost housing project, investigating the phenomenon of iridescence, where light reflects off the different layers of a substance, creating interference patterns that are expressed as shifting colour, for example as in petrol or a peacock's tail feathers. Radiant light film in structured layers was used within the facade. Metal oxides on the surface reflect light in different spectra depending on the angle of incidence and the angle of view. The effect is totally different in various weather conditions because the sky is a reciprocal surface. The strange film is held within dimpled cast-glass vitrines. A screen of silver birch trees throws fragments of indigo shade on to the facade. It is like a chemical flare, reminiscent of the cheap glory of Victorian match factories, dye works, sugar refineries, petrol dumps and Roses Primrose Soap.

Rose Window, Sherwood Forest, Nottingham, 2006
The two-storey high rose window here is made from computer-cut plywood flats which act as wind braces for a glass wall that is largely concealed beyond the timber reveals. The construction combines the complexity of computer cutting with the simplicity of halving joints in plywood to create something that has richness in its pattern but simplicity in its fabrication. The cellular structure of the screen is like the enlarged section of a stalk, made of cross-linked cellulose walls. On the north side of the building, the panels are infilled with glass, but on the south side they are filled with earth. Unrealised, the rose window proposal is currently being reconceived for a project in Ireland.

Delay, Soane Street Canopy, London, 2007

In this competition entry for a laminated canopy made from computer-etched copper sheet, each face of the copper is prepatinated using a different method before it is cut, so that, over time, the two layers will come to look quite different from each other. It is hoped that a clear, bright copper colour, a brown-purple patina and slowly emerging verdigris will develop, and that the structure will come into its own over a period of about a hundred years. The colours will mingle visually as the patinated, cut and folded layers interleave, and the canopy will cast shadows on to the black stone beneath. The stone is etched in a geometric pattern, so that the copper oxide in solution dripping down from above will create a green inlay pattern, staining the etched stone and running off the polished surface. The object, its halo, its shadow and its stained residue will interact in different patterns over short and long time periods. Thus screens are like clocks. ◬

Out of the Phase

Making an Approach to Architecture

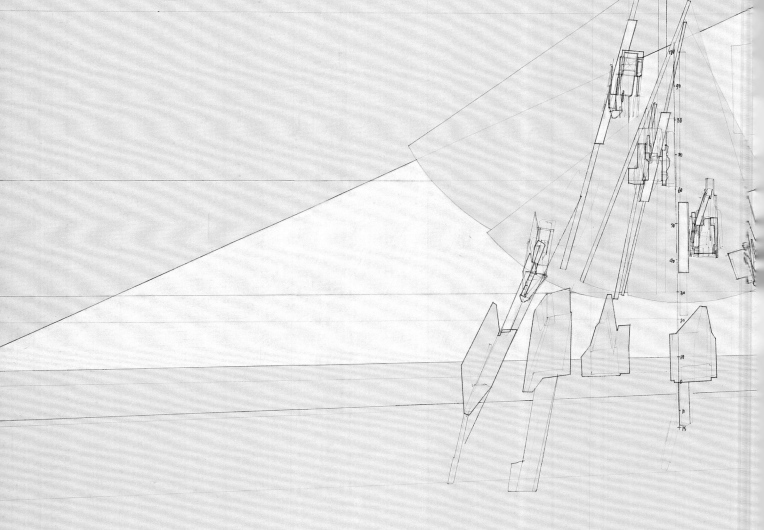

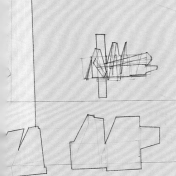

and Landscape

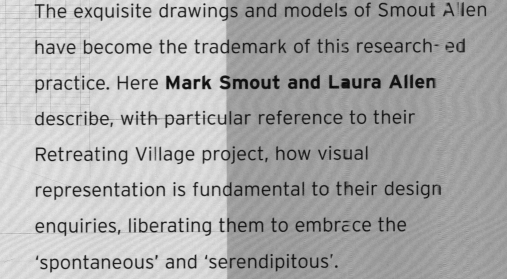

The exquisite drawings and models of Smout Allen have become the trademark of this research-ed practice. Here **Mark Smout and Laura Allen** describe, with particular reference to their Retreating Village project, how visual representation is fundamental to their design enquiries, liberating them to embrace the 'spontaneous' and 'serendipitous'.

Smout Allen, Village for a Retreating Landscape, Happisburgh, Norfolk, UK, 2005
Early sketch iteration. Ghosts of the lost houses are echoed in the Retreating Village. Houses begin to withdraw from the edge into a tight cluster via a framework of sliding skids, guide rails and winch systems.

The design process that leads from inception, through production to resolution is often far from linear, smooth or uninterrupted. It can exist instead as a series of more or less distinct phases of syncopated investigations, many of which are trialled and tested, scaled and exposed in three dimensions, while some, in contrast, remain nothing more than a thumbnail sketch. At the very least this is evidence of Smout Allen's desire to accumulate numerous potential avenues of interest, to draw out ideas from the imagination and to rouse latent influences along the way. This practice points to an evolutionary and generative process, in which each phase of development and divergent adaptation is crucial. Visual representation by means of drawings and models is a fundamental mode of design enquiry that provides, in varying degrees, a register of the investigation, the object of the investigation and its product. Drawings of this kind are not necessarily intended as an end in themselves; instead the drawing is a tool for the creative process from which things begin to take form.

The Retreating Village, an investigation into the shifting landscapes of north Norfolk, the erosion of its sea cliffs and the collapse of the village of Happisburgh into the sea, began with what became a series of pieces that examined the potential of the site and proposed a new architecture that could exist in these precarious coastal territories. The studies took a number of routes, such as working with the architectural languages of impermanence and temporality, new notions for inhabitation, responses to the results of climate change, architectural materiality, perceptual and optical environmental phenomena, the landscape in art and literature, and the manufacture and use of 'drawing' tools.

As a primary concern the study looked at a landscape that becomes dislocated from its surroundings. As the ground gives way beneath it, the indeterminably deep boundary of the horizon where sky and land meet is accentuated and the midgrounds and foregrounds blend together. The horizon line, although observable, seems an uninhabitable margin – objects here are fixed on to, rather than into, this depth of space. Its appearance is mutable: daily and seasonal fluctuations of light modify the colour and contrast of the sky and that of the objects that it touches.

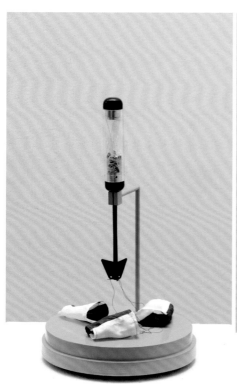

Ballistic device 1: net instrument. A weighted cap is released to allow a woven net of reflective nodes to be released into the air. Flight is stabilised and speed controlled by fins and drogue parachutes.

Ballistic device 2: glint instrument. Mirrored fins are attached to a central stabilising rod and a vacuum cylinder which pressure-releases and tilts the fins in flight.

Ballistic device 3: dynamic line instrument. A weighted cap detaches the Perspex outer casing and releases three sprung-steel tapes to deploy as lines in the sky. A canopy parachute brings the mechanism safely back to earth.

The Net Assemblage.

Three ballistic instruments were devised that could expose the nature of this ephemeral environment. Each has an implied functionality and performance, but unlike tools in the accepted sense, their usefulness is also measured in the making process – the choice and use of materials, their technical configuration, scale, weight and mounting. Their design begins to imply a taxidermal relationship with the object. Each is designed to inhabit the space between the sky and the ground. They are propelled up and outwards from a portable launcher with considerable accuracy, and deploy at a given height and speed where a split-second spatial event is triggered to reveal the nature of the sites they temporarily occupy. The instruments use shape, shine, shadow and silhouette to enable visual recognition of form, and consequently to examine the apparent depth of the horizon.

Camouflage strategies such as these, employed by nature and in the design of disruptive pattern materials to conceal an object within its environment, can in much the same way be designed to accentuate and reveal figure and position. A 'net' of reflective pieces infiltrates and plots the depth of the blurred or fractured horizon to reveal silhouettes as deep three-dimensional objects. The 'glint' instrument illuminates the distance of the horizon, momentarily foreshortening the three-dimensional space between foreground and background, while in midair mirrored fins are opened out and, for an instant, are tilted to flash to the observer. Thus varying intensities of reflectance are produced, depending on the triangulation of the fins, the viewer and the light source. The third instrument is specifically deployed in an urban environment where one is more intimately surrounded by an irregular and interrupted horizon. This instrument employs a dynamic line that rapidly unravels in flight. A line is literally drawn along the hard edge of the occupied sky.

The devices add to both an objective knowledge and the subjective experience of the horizon space, and are taken on to inform strategies for architectural concealment and revelation. Their performance and landscape are interpreted in three assemblages, conceived of as paintings, of light, metal and coloured film, which begin to suggest spatial and architectural propositions. They are presented backlit on a fluxing light-box which allows the paintings to be seen against the fluctuating balance of projected and reflected light. Subtle gradients of colour are thus revealed in the apparently flat black silhouettes.

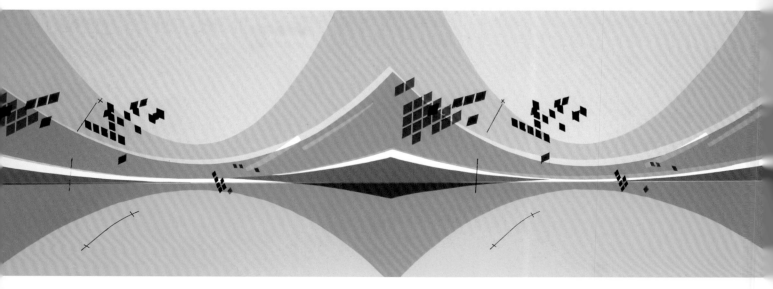

The Glint Assemblage.

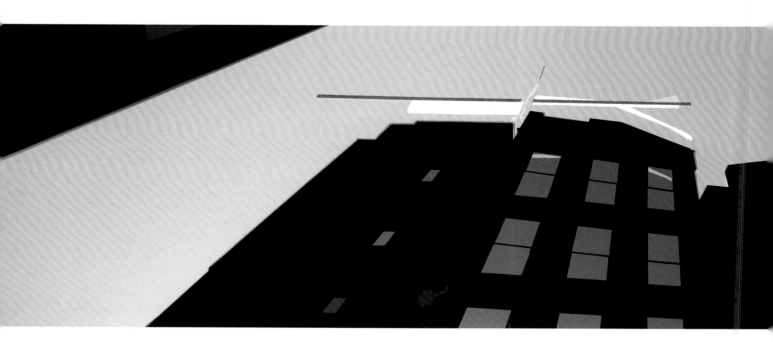

The Dynamic Line Assemblage.

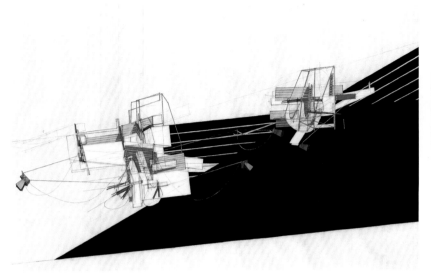

Single house configuration: scale 1:200.

Each house is accompanied by a succession of screens, armatures, pulleys, skids, decking, louvres and revetments that act as armour, selectively shielding or exposing the village to the wind, rain and sun. The architecture is specular in its responsiveness to the landscape.

In the Net Assemblage, layers of tree silhouettes are subtly coloured to create both an indeterminate surface and the illusion of depth. A laced net of silver wire infiltrates the trees and traces between the layers, which are punctuated with holes to channel unfiltered light through to the surface. The space of the fractured horizon is occupied by an array that acts as a focus for the image as one's eyes adjust to the varying background-light levels. The Glint Assemblage investigates the depth of the raised horizon, in this case the cliff top seen from the beach. Stereoscopic views place the edge in deep three-dimensional space. Layers of overlapping cut-out coloured film are animated in the Dynamic Line Assemblage by the perceivable variation between ambient and projected light to highlight the urban edge as it shifts from the compressed space of the silhouette to the topography of the city.

The topological rearrangement of the landscape incites a displacement and subsequent reconstruction of the site. The architecture of the village is formed here from a lexicon of pieces that coalesce into a variety of inhabitable spaces. The disintegrating cliff, the predicament of the environment and a mapping of a new village that is able to retreat away from the edge is drawn in a series of large aerial views. Their aspect is neither orthographic nor perspectival, but instead each drawing uses a combination of viewpoints, and occasionally long and multiple exposures, to illustrate and chart the temporality of the site. The architecture, perceived as an event in the landscape, is rendered as a panoramic observation. Such techniques are more commonly associated with photography and landscape painting than architectural drawings, which are at times cumbersome and limiting as a mode of representation. The drawings here are worked concurrently with the ballistic devices, and ideas migrate between them.

Design through drawing and making can be considered a haptic experience where the physical act of piecing together ideas in two and three dimensions allows one to come into close contact with the very matter of the problem. This is especially relevant in a design approach that is not entirely question led where one hopes to provoke a freethinking attitude that allows for and embraces spontaneous and serendipitous events. ◭

Objects after Image

For 12 years, the Koshirakura Landscape Workshop has been an annual summer event. Located in a beautiful and remote region of Japan, it encourages a small group of architecture students to respond to the setting by creating projects that read, represent and spatially reconfigure the landscape into new constructions. Shin Egashira reveals how, over time, these constructions in turn act as a continuous form of documentation and reflection.

If Alice had been asked: 'What will change when objects appear smaller?'
She might have replied: 'The distance between them, or the number of wrinkles.'

If Alice had been asked: 'What will remain when objects disappear?'
She might have replied: 'Afterimage.'

Koshirakura village lies some 200 kilometres (124 miles) north of Tokyo, and is one of 13 villages scattered along the complex terrains of the Shibumi River. The village is an exceptionally active micro-community that is resisting the process of erasure affecting the rural landscape of Japan. Sublime and fragile images of 'place' and 'life expression' are but one side of a coin that reflects the contemporary city in construction as its other side.

The Koshirakura Landscape Workshop was founded in 1996, and has as its base the former local elementary school that had lain idle since 1994 due to insufficient numbers of local school-age children. In association with the local government, the workshop soon became an annual event. Every summer, a small group of international architecture students arrives and sets up shop. The programme has three stages: the reading and repeated rereading of the landscape; the representation of the landscape from details and materials, allowing for the reinterpretation of reality

Koshirakura Landscape Workshop, Cinema screen, Koshirakura, Niigata Prefecture, Japan, 2004
top: The cinema screen functions as a gateway to the annual Momijihiki (maple-tree cutting) Festival.
centre: The components of the timber screen.
bottom: The landscape is clearly visible through the screen in daylight, but at dusk fades to a silhouette ready for projection.

Koshirakura Landscape Workshop Axonometric, 1996–2007
opposite: All the details and parts of the buildings constructed over the workshop's 12-year period are reimagined linked together.

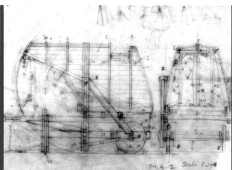

Slow Box/After Image, Echigo Tsumari Art Triennial, Niigata Prefecture, Japan, 2000
1:20 construction section.

1:20 timber carcass model horizontal (darkroom) position.

1:20 timber carcass model upright (camera) position.

In July, a local tractor in Takakura village became the Slow Box's means of mobility.

The Slow Box in Takakura village.

Slow Box communal self-portrait session in Funasaka village.

from different viewpoints; and the rearranging of these details into new forms of spatial construction.

In this sense, the act of making buildings becomes a continuous form of documentation and reflection, as well as a direct means of design experimentation. Built form is not determined from the outset. Components are often made and possible scales discovered by repeating inherent patterns of detail in different sizes and proportions. Over the past 12 years, a total of 16 built projects including a bus shelter, pavilion, cinema screen and viewing platform, and other artefacts including films and maps, have been completed with very limited resources and minimal facilities by adapting anything available as a tool, and mixing various techniques and materials. In recent years the work has begun to suggest alternative notions of recycling and reuse. This not only applies to materials and land, but also to the stories and memories of the villagers. Filming is not only appropriated as a means of recording the temporality of built projects; it is assembled to construct a sense of fiction.

Real Fiction

In 2004 the workshop made a film, *Real Fiction*, by reinventing its constructions as props and stages. Working methods included site-specific location shooting, editing on camera, making new props, writing film scripts, acting and editing clips on laptops, and at the same time searching for good sandstone for foundations, mixing concrete, making timber details with saws and chisels, and collecting local stories. Ropes were stretched to make a screen, and a small shrine was made to protect an expensive data projector borrowed from the town hall. On the eve of the annual Momijihikl (maple-tree cutting) Festival of Koshirakura, sitting on the stone steps leading up to the shrine entrance, waiting for our film to begin, we watched the landscape visible through the screen become a silhouette as the sun set behind it and then was gradually overlapped and replaced by our film scenes in electric blue, glowing ever more brightly in the increasing darkness. When the wind blew through the screen of ropes the image vibrated, causing a sense of movement and immediacy.

Slow Box and After Image

In 2000, it was decided to stage the first international art triennial in the Tsumari District of Niigata. Its director, Fram Kitagawa of the Art Front Gallery, invited 136 artists from 32 nations to take part in the event, and I was invited to submit a proposal for an art work that would form links between seven towns and cities across the district. The idea evolved into a three-stage project. The first stage involved making an object, the Slow Box, that would register the climate and aspects of the various towns and cities. The second stage used the Slow Box as a vehicle to communicate with local residents, and the third stage involved making an installation to document the passage of the vehicle and communication events (After Image). The result was the fabrication of a large pinhole camera vehicle, large enough to accommodate a person, which would travel through the villages of Tsumari once every three years.

The size of the vehicle was determined by the proportional relationship between objects, the size of the picture plane, the diameter of the aperture and the distance between them. This required an exposure time of between 15 and 30 minutes in typical daylight conditions. The direct print (imprint) size is 1.5 x 1.5 metres (4.9 x 4.9 feet) on a 5-millimetre (0.2-inch) toughened-glass pane coated with photo emulsion. The itinerary was determined by asking each town to recommend its most beautiful village/community in a difficult-to-reach location. Seven villages showed their interest in collaborating, namely Takakura, Takizawa, Kurokura, Kettou, Seitayama, Funasaka and Koshirakura. With three to four days in each village, the journey therefore became a 'documentary of documenting' over a total of 24 days.

Slow Box Kurokura village portrait. A 1.5 x 1.5 metre (4.9 x 4.9 foot) composite contact print on 5-millimetre (0.2-inch) thick float-glass negatives – one of a series of 27 such After Image composites captured by Slow Box on its journey in 2000.

After Image archive: installation in Takakura village, August 2000
Here, 1.5 x 1.5 metre (4.9 x 4.9 foot), 5-millimetre (0.2-inch) thick float-glass negatives weighing 25 kilograms (55 pounds) each were extracted from the Slow Box, one at a time after each exposure, and then developed in the darkroom. A series of 27 landscape portraits captured by Slow Box during its 24-day journey in 2000 formed a public room inside a disused school gym in Takakura village. The glass negatives acted as light filters, reflecting the sunlight and casting shadows as After Image slowly moved across the floor at different angles throughout the day.

Baby Slow Box, Echigo Tsumari Art Triennial, Niigata Prefecture, Japan, 2003
Baby Slow Box is a suitcase that unfolds into a wearable camera, and was made to accompany Slow Box on its 2003 journey.

Baby Slow Box

In 2003, a baby-size Slow Box travelled in tandem with the original Slow Box along the same passage and on the same date as it had in 2000. With its smaller size allowing access to narrow paths, gardens, front entrances and living rooms, it provided new backgrounds for different types of portraits: of small local groups, couples and individuals who were able to relate their personal stories of the making of their interior landscapes. Baby Slow Box is made from a suitcase, a folding baby buggy, an overcoat and a 10-millimetre (0.4-inch) diameter magnifying lens for its eye, which blinks at preselected intervals of between 2 and 180 seconds.

The idea of a transfigurative wearable camera was initially inspired by Michael Webb's Cushicle (air CUSHion vehiCLE) mobile environment that enables an individual to carry a complete environment on his or her back. The challenge was then to adapt such a concept in a remote, rural environment without power or fuel. The resulting adaptable camera became a structure that was worn, and thus took on the behavioural characteristics of the carrier. It also had the quality of a toy or toddler's gadget, in so far as it generated a playful experience of looking at our immediate surroundings. The slow and careful ritual of transforming the assembly into a camera, positioning the subject, setting exposure duration, fixing distance, adjusting scale and framing the background recast the sublime and personal relationship between body and landscape.

Fabricated and tested in London, the Baby Slow Box took an economy passenger flight to Narita airport to be united with its larger predecessor. ⧋

Project credits
Koshirakura Landscape Workshop, Real Fiction, 2004: Xenia Adjoubei, Rubens Azedebo, Mei Chan, Hiroshi Eguchi, Panos Hadjichristofis, Rita Lee, Ryan Kwong Hung Li, Angela Lim, Sandra del Missier, Matthew Murphy, Maryam Pousti, Marike Schoonderbeck, Hyun-Young Sung, Chikako Takahashi, Shing On Evonne Tam, Nogol Zahabi.

Slow Box/After Image Journey, Echigo Tsumari Art Triennial, 2000: Ema Bonafacic, Maria Chung, Phoebe Dakin, Suk-Kyu Hong, Koichi Ioka, Anna Kubelic, Aoi Kome, Julia Mauser, Inigo Minns, Shuji Murakami, Bart Schoonderbeck, Demos Simatos, Yasushi Takahashi, Kazuhiro Igawa.

Slow Box/After Image Journey, Echigo Tsumari Art Triennial, 2003: Farah Azizan, Sarah Entwistle, Ko Matoba, Akiharu Ogino, Adrian Priestman, Adiam Sertzu, Anna Shevel, Lena Tutunjian, Ottilie Ventiroso, Chen Zhi Xion,

Family portraits; the 40 x 60-centimetre (15.7 x 23.6-inch) contact prints are two of a series of 10 such After Image composites captured by Baby Slow Box in 2003.

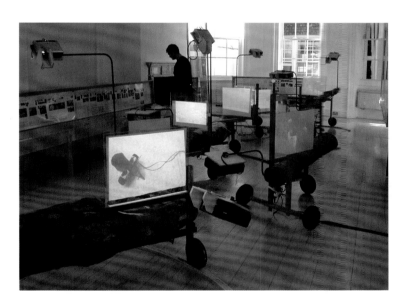

Before Object After Image: installation at the Architectural Association, London, October 2007
The installation was accompanied by the AA publication Before Object After Image and documented and reviewed the workshop's 12 years of direct responses to the given context of a post-agricultural community in transition. Following the tradition of Koshirakura's tree-cutting ritual, a birch was installed inside the gallery. The cuts in the tree seen here were dictated by the geometry of the Koshirakura landscape and the mapping of the coordinates of all the built projects. The seven sections of trunk set off on their journey equipped with legs on wheels. Each section houses a projector displaying 2,400 images and three films from the workshops.

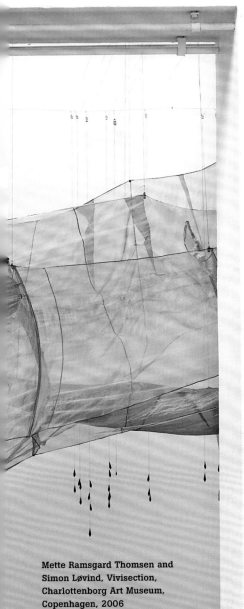

Robotic
Membranes

Exploring a Textile
Architecture of
Behaviour

Mette Ramsgard Thomsen and
Simon Løvind, Vivisection,
Charlottenborg Art Museum,
Copenhagen, 2006

The robot and the textile seem like a contradiction in terms – the robot standing for everything that is automated and mechanical, and the textile for sensual materiality. Can it be possible to reconcile the two? Here **Mette Ramsgard Thomsen** demonstrates through her Vivisections and Strange Metabolisms projects, exhibited at the Centre for Information, Technology and Architecture (CITA) in Copenhagen, how it is possible to unite the seeming polarities of the digital and the physical, engaging 'intangible digital data with tactile physical material'.

The relationship between digital and analogue is often constructed as one of opposition. The perception that the world is permeated with underlying patterns of data, describing events and matter alike, suggests that information can be understood apart from the substance to which it is associated, and that its encoded logic can be constructed and reconfigured as an isolated entity. This disembodiment of information from materiality implies that an event like a thunderstorm, or a material like a body, can be described equally by data, in other words it can be read or written.

The following prototypes, Vivisection and Strange Metabolisms, were developed at the Centre for Information Technology and Architecture (CITA) at the Royal Danish Academy of Fine Arts in Copenhagen as a means of engaging intangible digital data with tactile physical material. As robotic membranes, they are a dual examination of computational and material interfaces. By considering these ideas at an architectural scale, the Robotic Membranes project examines how walls, floors and ceilings of the built environment may be regarded as dynamic surfaces acting and reacting to changes of containment, and the contained.

In robotics, digital logics are tied to a physical body through the relationship between sensing and actuation. Thus the computed is always connected to its environment, to the structure and gravity of its body, and its situation in context.

In Robotic Membranes, sensing is linked to actuation through a textile surface. Using textile as a technology as well as a material, the membrane is understood as a means of assemblage, allowing the bespoke specking of complex surfaces.

Weaving, knitting, lacing and felting are technologies that gather separate fibres in order to engineer unified materials with particular local properties. In Robotic Membranes, integrated conductive fibres such as steel threads and carbon-loaded fibres allow the passing of data through the weave, while at the same time using the pliable nature of textiles to enable actuation. The resulting robotic membrane merges the structural properties of architectural enclosure with the variable data of its environment, and once embedded with control potential allows us to propose programmable and dynamic architecture.

Vivisection

Vivisection is the first prototype in the making of a robotic membrane, and is a collaboration between architect Mette Ramsgard Thomsen and designer Simon Løvind. Vivisection is the making of a live section, a sensing skin that acts and reacts to inhabitation. As a spatial experiment it investigates, firstly, the means of embedding capacity for sensing and actuation within a tectonic surface and, secondly, how intelligent programming paradigms might generate a sense of spatial autonomy from occupation and use. Vivisection is a large-scale installation that defines an interior and an exterior, as well as a volume that escapes inhabitation yet, through the scale of its cavities, relates to the body. Inspired by large-scale textile constructions such as box kites and parachutes, it is constructed from three connected sections that create separate interior chambers. The chambers are inhabited by three 'lungs' which, through their continuous inhalations and exhalations, give the construction an inherent movement and rhythm.

Mette Ramsgard Thomsen and Simon Løvind, Vivisection, Charlottenborg Art Museum, Copenhagen, 2006
Vivisection is made from an organza of silk and steel. The steel weft is conductive, which allows the passing of electronic data through it. The lungs have a silicone coating creating a composite material that can be inflated and deflated.

In Robotic Membranes, integrated conductive fibres such as steel threads and carbon-loaded fibres allow the passing of data through the weave, while at the same time using the pliable nature of textiles to enable actuation.

Vivisection uses a conductive organza as its core material. The organza is a weave of steel and silk. The steel weft is conductive, which allows the passing of electronic signals through it. By connecting an antenna-based sensor chip to the fabric, the material becomes sensitive as it registers changes in the magnetic field around the antennae. As users touch or pass underneath the fabric, they actuate an embedded sensor. A microprocessor subsequently instructs a series of fans to inflate or deflate the assembly's lungs, whose fabric was treated with silicone making the material airtight and inflatable. The silicone also makes the lungs heavy, causing them to collapse when the fans are switched off. Finally, a copper 'nerve path' has been embroidered along the length of the installation allowing the material to pass information between a total of three microprocessors that control the entire installation. As such, Vivisection becomes a sensitive skin that actively engages its inhabitation. The fabric becomes a composite material combining the properties of conductivity, inflate-ability and deflate-ability. It also becomes an interface in which the assembly knows about its environment and communicates its understanding to itself.

Vivisection queries the programming of architecture by adopting computation as a distributed event. The robotic membrane acts as a matrix enabling the communication of multiple cells. Each cell is both independent and relational by acting and reacting to input from its immediate environment as well as that of other cells elsewhere on the membrane. The resulting rhythm of the installation represents the collective and local response of each cell, generating complexity through their overlay. From this bottom-up strategy, reactive behaviours emerge, creating an inherent indeterminacy within the structure. Robotic Membranes asks how computation of environmental behaviour can drive and change behaviour in physical material. It also examines the emergence of behavioural patterns, such as repetition. And it asks how architectural material may give, stretch or deform in such a way as to affect its own motility and presence.

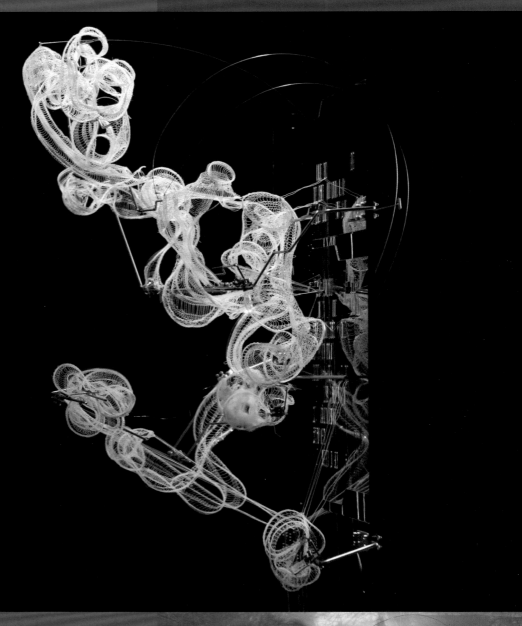

Mette Ramsgard Thomsen and Toni Hicks, Strange Metabolisms, Grand Parade Gallery, Brighton, 2007
Strange Metabolisms uses complex knit structures to make bespoke three-dimensional membranes. The models are animated through dynamic armatures allowing the membranes to collapse and expand the spaces they suggest.

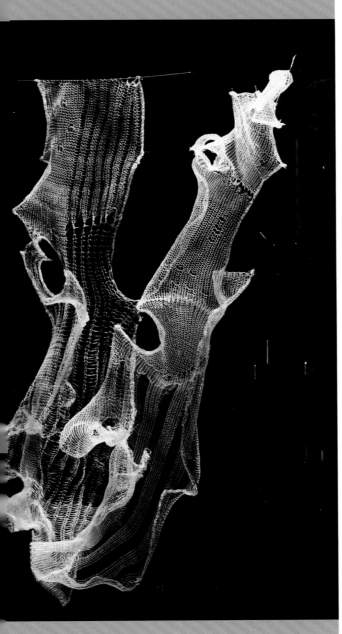

Strange Metabolisms

The second prototype, Strange Metabolisms, speculates on how the bespoke shaping of a membrane prescribes a particular sense of motility. Developed in collaboration with knitter Toni Hicks of Constructed Textiles at the University of Brighton, Strange Metabolisms investigates how knit as a principle of construction can lead to new formal as well as behavioural languages. It operates at scale 1:50, and the models are machine-knitted structures, merging synthetic as well as natural fibres such as plastic, silk, steel and wool, and using the strength and qualities of these fibres to design bespoke skins that change according to their site and occupation.

Strange Metabolisms makes use of the inherent three-dimensionality of knit as a tectonic structure. The models develop surfaces that extend tubular knitting techniques, known from socks and gloves, as well as simple double-knit structures creating complex surfaces with protrusions, folds, layerings and slits. Furthermore, stitch sizes are scaled, changing the density, flex and structural integrity of the material as well as its porosity and translucence. By integrating conductive and resistive fibres, parts of the surfaces can be actuated with heat changes and the switching on and off of embedded LED lights.

Strange Metabolisms is a further speculation on movement and change in Robotic Membranes in which ways of integrating smart memory alloys and smart memory polymers into the knitted structures are investigated. In these test pieces, the membrane is actuated through the state change of the integrated smart material. Here, the scale of actuation and the scale of the project become intrinsically linked.

Conclusion

By engaging the computational with the material, Robotic Membranes examines the possibilities for complex interrelationships between the encoded and the actual. Vivisection and Strange Metabolisms explore how the specking of a material surface with an intelligent weave offers the possibility for space to be activated and behavioural. They also explore and develop ways in which sensing and actuation may be integrated into architectural surfaces. Such responsive systems may be seen as parallel and dynamic auxiliaries to the usually static quality of spatial enclosures, their structure, form, colour, opacity and so on. Both the Vivisection and Strange Metabolisms prototypes create a lab environment for the exploration of how a reactive surface can be imagined. Regarding enclosure as a live and active entity, Robotic Membranes asks how concepts such as distributed computing and intelligent programming can allow for the emergence of complex behaviours. It suggests that we may seek to build beyond the static, and design spaces that evolve across time. ⊡

The concepts and technologies of Strange Metabolisms were developed through a series of workshops run by collaborators architect Mette Ramsgard Thomsen and knitter Toni Hicks, here with students from the Royal Danish Academy of Fine Arts School of Architecture and Textiles Design in Copenhagen.

Mapping the Invisible Landscape

An Exercise in Spatially Choreographed Sound

Paul Bavister of Audialsense describes
how a series of auditory research
installations in the Turbine Hall of the
Tate Modern presented the opportunity to
play with the relationship between sound
and the built, inverting the usual
relationship in which architecture
accommodates the acoustic.

Audialsense, '100hertz', Tate Modern,
Bankside, London, April 2007
The Turbine Hall interior.

Beginning the walk down the ramp of the Turbine Hall to
get a feel for where the standing waves occurred.

The site of the installation showing speakers located
on the steps along the side of the Turbine Hall.

Recording the pulse of the standing waves on a digital sound recorder from a fixed position.

When sound is reflected off a room boundary, the reflected wave interacts with the incident wave causing constructive and destructive interference patterns.

The physical relationship between architecture and sound has been practised throughout history. The built-in 'resonant chambers' in the walls of ancient theatres and temples, and the Denge sound mirrors near Dungeness in Kent are but two examples of how the physics of sound influences the shape of the built environment. However, this relationship can be turned on its head, and an acoustic environment that has been shaped by the built can emerge as 'unseen architecture', never previously considered or imagined by its original designers.

Since its conversion from a power station in May 2000 by Herzog & de Meuron, the Turbine Hall at Tate Modern on London's Bankside has established itself as one of the world's most important cultural landmarks. Its cavernous interior has hosted some of the largest interior installations ever produced, and as such each Unilever-sponsored project is highly anticipated due to the challenge of this scale. For one evening on 5 April 2007, Audialsense (Paul Bavister, Jason Flanagan and Ian Knowles) were given access to the vast space of the Turbine Hall to conduct a series of auditory research installations looking at the spatial effects of 'pure sound' within such a large volume, effects that could be experienced audibly, and physically due to the large pressure differentials inherent in standing waves.

Sound is made up of travelling pressure waves. Externally, sound levels diminish with distance as the energy is dissipated. The interaction of sound with architecture brings about a much more complex situation. When sound is reflected off a room boundary, the reflected wave interacts with the incident wave causing constructive and destructive interference patterns.

Standing waves may be created from the collision of two waves (with equal frequency and wavelength) travelling in opposite directions. The net result alternates between zero and a maximum amplitude, unlike the travelling waves. In a room, the locations of these maxima and minima are stationary and can be both predicted and experienced physically.

Standing wave phenomena can also occur in a room at specific frequencies, often referred to as resonance frequencies, which are dependent on the dimension and shape of the space. At resonance, the acoustic response of the room will be enhanced. Resonance frequencies are defined as room modes, and depending upon how many of the room boundaries are involved, they are termed axial, tangential or oblique, with axial modes being the strongest.

The fundamental mode is the frequency corresponding to the lowest whole wavelength that can be accommodated in a space, and so there is a fundamental frequency that corresponds to the length, width and height of a room. Multiples of the fundamental are called harmonics.

So when standing waves occur at sufficient volume, they become perceivable by physical means, the air densities of the waves being higher than normal air pressure, so that the appearance of walking into, and out of, the sound is apparent. As these waves appear spatially according to the modal characteristics of the room, it is important for designers to understand how these

The sonic landscape formed
by the standing waves in the
occupied zone of the hall.

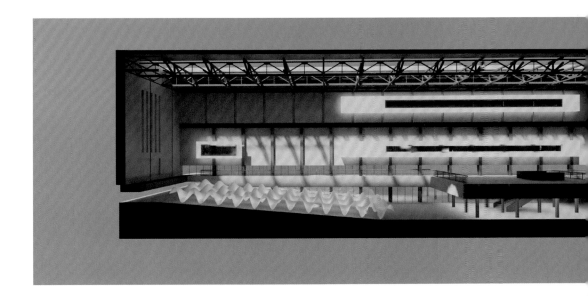

Longitudinal section through the Turbine Hall showing the distribution pattern of the standing waves.

invisible patterns manifest themselves. How do we interact with an invisible landscape of differing air densities, and can such a landscape be visualised?

From transformers in an adjacent (working) power station, sited at either end of the Turbine Hall, a 100-hertz hum is emitted. This hum is omnipresent, and varies only by a few hertz over time, a fluctuation that is modulated by the activities of the people living and working around the gallery who draw on the electricity supply.

In the first installation, Audialsense first played back a pure 100-hertz tone into the gallery to counter the existing tone. The effect was twofold. Initially there was silence. Even though 100 hertz at considerable volume was being played into the hall, there was none of the familiar auditory evidence of this. However, on mapping the locations of standing waves, the volume became apparent: one only had to move slightly to find oneself in a deafening ball of volume. The effect was quite unsettling, a very loud and physical experience, even encouraging clothes to flap! Most spectacular was the incredible interference that occurred when the hall's existing 100-hertz hum dropped a few hertz due to activity in the local area. The hall seemed to slowly groan and shudder, before settling back into its 100-hertz equilibrium.

The Turbine Hall measures approximately 152 metres (498.7 feet) long, 30 metres (98.4 feet) high and 24 metres (78.7 feet) wide, dimensions that correspond to wavelengths of 2.2 hertz, 11.3 hertz and 14.1 hertz. When scaled in a purely mathematical ratio, the pitch of the sine waves enters into the realm of human hearing, and formed a site-specific chord, which was then held for a long time to allow standing waves to be formed

within the space. The standing waves were also site specific, and were physically perceived/experienced. Audialsense then introduced scrolling sine waves into the space. These are waves that rise and fall in pitch between two set parameters, which in this case were defined by the extremes of the human voice, both male and female. As the two 'gender-specific' waves gently oscillated, they passed the static waves as defined by the room, causing interference and beating (rhythmic pulses of sound).

All buildings have an element of 'noise' that exists within their walls. A building's infrastructure acts a conduit/sounding board for all the bumps, squeaks and groans that general occupancy generates, and such sounds can be captured by accelerometers. Using the previously defined site-specific 'chord', Audialsense next added elements of structure-borne noise into the mix, finally hearing the building as defined by both spatial and physical qualities.

In order to establish the locations of the standing waves during each of the installations, a number of walks were taken through the hall along a predetermined route of equal length and time with a digital sound recorder. The recordings were then uploaded to a computer and visualised using basic frequency and spectral analysis software, which revealed the fluctuations in sound pressure during each individual installation. As the walks were identical in time and length, any shift in the analysis data indicated a changed location of standing-wave phenomena. Longitudinal and lateral standing waves at 100 hertz were identified, the acoustic response of the Turbine Hall being a series of pools of constructive and destructive interference revealing a landscape of sound that is dramatically opposed to the regular, linear nature of the architecture. ∆

The results of these experiments were presented at the Sonic Arts Networks annual conference in Plymouth in 2007. Audialsense would like to thank Tate Modern and JBL speakers for their kind support of this project.

Contributors

Laura Allen and **Mark Smout** are lecturers in architecture at the Bartlett School of Architecture, UCL, London. Their research projects scrutinise and interpret the fluxing urban and rural landscape and its reaction and adaptation to natural environmental events and the 'artificial' influence of man. They have recently published *Augmented Landscapes*, the latest in the renowned Pamphlet Architecture series published by Princeton Architectural Press, and in 2005 their work was awarded Best in Show at the Royal Academy of Arts Summer Exhibition by the AJ/Bovis Awards judging panel.

Audialsense (www.audialsense.com) is a collective of architects and sound artists established in 2005 and comprises **Paul Bavister**, Jason Flanagan and acoustician Ian Knowles. Based in London, they have executed a series of spatially related sound installations in and around the capital. The team regularly lecture on their work at universities, and in 2007 presented a paper on the Turbine Hall experiments at the Sonic Arts Network's annual conference in Plymouth.

Marcos Cruz and **Marjan Colletti** are founders of marcosandmarjan, and are both lecturers in architecture at the Bartlett School of Architecture, UCL (Unit 20), and the University of Westminster (DS10). Their individual and joint work, as well as their student projects, has been widely published and exhibited, including at the 'Actions re Form' exhibition in Coimbra and Munich (2002), the São Paulo Biennial (2003) and the Venice Biennale (2004). In 2005 they published *Marcosandmarjan: Interfaces/Intrafaces*, a comprehensive monograph of their work, as part of the Springer's iCP Consequence Book Series on Fresh Architecture.

Kate Davies and **Emmanuel Vercruysse** of LIQUID FACTORY seek to inhabit the periphery of architecture; the points where it touches the related disciplines of art and performance. They are primarily concerned with the event. Viewing a site as a territory or stage for a series of performances, they seek interventions that respond to both spatial and temporal contexts. Both graduated from the Bartlett School of Architecture, UCL, in 2005. Vercruysse lectures at the Bartlett, and Davies works for the design practice Metaphor and is a part-time lecturer at Chelsea College of Art and Design.Their Prosthetic Mythologies project was undertaken during a residency awarded to LIQUID FACTORY by the Kielder Art and Architecture Partnership, Northumbria.

Evan Douglis is the principal of Evan Douglis Studio, an internationally renowned architecture and interdisciplinary design firm. The firm's unique cutting-edge research into computer-aided digital design and fabrication technology, new materials, multimedia installations and, more recently, a new generation of building components as applied to a range of diverse projects, has elicited international acclaim. Douglas has received numerous awards including an NYFA Grant, *Architectural Record*'s Design Vanguard Award, and an ACADIA Award for Emerging Digital Practice. He was also a Finalist Nominee for the North American James Beard Foundation Restaurant Design Awards. His work has been published in *Sign as Surface, INDEX Architecture, The State of Architecture at the Beginning of the 21st Century, 10 x10_2, Distinguishing Digital Architecture: 6th Far Eastern International Design Award, FURNISH: Furniture and Interior Design for the 21st Century,* and *Architecture Now 5*. He is currently the chair of the Undergraduate School of Architecture at Pratt Institute. www.evandouglis.com

Shin Egashira has taught at the Architectural Association, London, since 1990, and is currently Unit Master of Diploma Unit 11. His art works and installations have been exhibited worldwide, and his most recent project, How to Walk a Flat Elephant, was created in collaboration with Okamura Furniture Corporation in Tokyo. He also conducts a series of landscape workshops in rural communities across the world including, Koshirakura village in Niigata Prefecture, Japan, Gu-Zhu village in Yong Ding, China, and Muxagata town on the northern edge of Portugal.

Stephen Gage is a professor of innovative technology at the Bartlett School of Architecture, UCL. His professional career spans the design and construction of buildings, academic teaching and research in government, private practice and academic contexts. He currently coordinates the technical aspects of design research at the Bartlett, and is a founder member of the Bartlett Interactive Architecture Workshop. His current research focuses on the way in which the technology of building can subtly modify the internal environment, and the time-based aspects of architecture that relate to human occupation and building use. His many published buildings are recognised as leaders in their field.

Theo Jansen studied technical science in Delft, the Netherlands, yet he became a painter. Since 1990 he has been occupied with making new forms of life. His beach animals are made not from pollen or seeds, but from plastic yellow tubes. He is a columnist for the Dutch national newspaper *Volkskrant*, and articles about his work have been published in the *New Scientist, Wired* and *Popular Science*. His 2002 exhibition at the Kunsthal in Rotterdam drew 14,000 visitors. He has also written three books about technical art and evolution. In addition, several of his television appearances have encouraged thousands of people to go to the beach to see him working there.

Niall McLaughlin was born in Geneva and educated at University College Dublin. He graduated in 1984 and worked with Scott Tallon Walker in Dublin and London for five years. In 1990 he set up his own practice, combining professional work with teaching at UCL where he is a visiting professor. His practice carries out work in the UK, Europe and the US. He won Young British Architect of the Year in 1998, and was made a fellow of the RIAI for Architectural Achievement in 2000. In 2004, his house in West Cork won the Stephen Lawrence Prize for the best building by a UK practice with a budget under £1 million. His practice is currently one of five representing London in the Gritty Brits exhibition touring American museums. He has been external examiner at the University of Cambridge and the University of Edinburgh, and is chair of the RIBA Awards Group.

Mette Ramsgard Thomsen is an architect who specialises in interactive technologies. She is Associate Professor at the Danish Royal Academy of Fine Arts School of Architecture in Copenhagen, where she heads the Centre for Information Technology and Architecture (CITA). Her research centres on the design of spaces that are informed by the intersections between the digital and the material. Through a focus on intelligent programming and ideas of emergence, she explores how computational logics can lead to new spatial concepts. Her research is practice led, and through projects such as Robotic Membranes, Lacer, Sea Unsea and The Changing Room she investigates the design and realisation of a behavioural space. She has also researched and taught at the Bartlett School of Architecture, the Department of Computer Science at UCL, the Fraunhofer Institute and the University of Brighton School of Architecture and Design, and holds a PhD in architecture and computer science from UCL.

Bob Sheil is an architect and a senior lecturer at the Bartlett School of Architecture, UCL. He has worked as a designer and maker in architecture, furniture, exhibition and web design. Following 10 years in practice, his teaching career began in the Bartlett workshop in 1995 where his key interest in, and curiosity about, the relationship between architecture and making evolved from practice to research. He is a founder member of the workshop-based practice sixteen*(makers) with Nick Callicott, Phil Ayres and Chris Leung. Since 2004 he has been programme director of the Bartlett's Graduate Diploma in Architecture, and in 2005 he guest-edited *AD Design through Making*.

Mark West is the founding director of the Centre for Architectural Structures and Technology (CAST), an associate professor of architecture at the University of Manitoba, and the inventor of numerous fabric formwork techniques. His research is founded in an art practice of drawing and sculpture, and in his education as an architect and builder.

Lebbeus Woods is an architect, teacher and critic whose work focuses on experimentation and the critical transformations of buildings, cities and landscapes. Monographs on his work include *Anarchitecture: Architecture is a Political Act* (St Martins Press, 1992), *Radical Reconstruction* (Princeton Architectural Press, 1997), *The Storm and the Fall* (Princeton Architectural Press, 2004) and *System Wien* (Hatje Cantz, 2005). His work is in public collections including the Museum of Modern Art, the Whitney Museum of American Art, and the Getty Research Institute for the Arts and Humanities in Los Angeles. He is the recipient of an American Institute of Architects Honours Award, the Chrysler Award for Innovation in Design, and the American Academy of Arts and Letters Award for Architecture. He has been a visiting professor at the Bartlett School of Architecture, UCL, SCI-ARC, Columbia University and Harvard University. He is currently a visiting professor at Pratt Institute, and a professor of architecture at the Cooper Union, New York.

AD+

Well-MADE
New York City
Apartments

Two New York City apartments redesigned
by the Brooklyn-based practice MADE
demonstrate how an architect's ability to
manufacture components and manage
construction can provide an unusual
quality of consistency and detail.
Jayne Merkel explains how the
apartments, which both owners purchased
for the views, have been transformed in
very different ways with a rare sensitivity
to the clients' needs and desires.

The three young partners at MADE who completely redesigned and rebuilt Apartment 25C were delighted to hear the owner say at the outset: 'I assume we need to take a wrecking ball to it.' Oliver Freundlich, Ben Bischoff and Brian Papa had founded their practice only two years earlier with design studios, a construction management department and a factory to build their designs. They had met at the Yale School of Architecture which all three attended at least partly because of the Yale Building Project – an unusual aspect of the curriculum that requires students to actually build something (usually a low-cost house or apartments) during the first year. Such hands-on experience changes the way students think during the entire three-year graduate programme. In their case, the interest in construction led to the unusual practice they created in 2000.

The MADE partners had a chance to put all their skills to work on Apartment 25C, which was finished in 2003, because the owners, like their other best clients, had previous experience with renovations. The three-bedroom, 158-square-metre (1,700-square-foot) apartment in a big, bulky 1986 building on Broadway and 68th Street serves as a pied-à-terre for a couple from the West Coast. The unit has long-range views of both Lincoln Center and Central Park, but it had a cramped awkward plan and bland detailing. Since the owners lived in a very curvaceous modern house in San Diego, they wanted everything to be very rectangular in New York, even though the apartment had a curved window on the prominent southwest corner.

The architects' wrecking ball removed all the interior walls as well as the kitchen, closets and three bathrooms. The ceiling was dropped in order to conceal lighting, wiring and pipes, and a new wall running the entire length of the apartment across from the outer window wall contains parts of the kitchen, two bathrooms, closets and mechanical

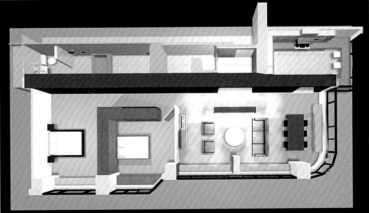

MADE, Apartment 25C, Broadway and 68th Street, Upper West Side, Manhattan, New York City, 2003
The storage walls inserted in Apartment 25C create an unusually uncluttered plan.

A curved element on the southeast corner of the living and dining areas is not echoed in the rigidly rectangular but very open, efficient and rigorous plan. The kitchen is behind the shiny dark wall on the left.

**MADE, Apartment 25C, Broadway and 68th Street,
Upper West Side, Manhattan, New York City, 2003**
A new shiny dark-brown wall runs the entire length of
Apartment 25C incorporating closets, mechanicals,
bathrooms and parts of the kitchen on the left. Bedrooms
and living areas are on the right (southern) side facing
an almost continuous band of tall windows.

A white-oak storage wall divides the guest and
master bedrooms. The same quarter-sawn, linear,
white-oak panelling also covers the entry walls.

The guest bathroom is housed in the shiny brown wall. Its cast-concrete tub serves as the base of the shower in the master bathroom on the other side of the opaque glass wall.

Cast-concrete countertops continue around the east end of the kitchen to create a breakfast area with views of Central Park.

equipment. The architects also added storage under the windows, in the wall that separates the two bedrooms from the back hall, and on a partition wall between the main living spaces and the private area with the bedrooms and baths; there is no clutter anywhere and very little freestanding furniture.

On the living room side, the partition wall, with a long thin cabinet attached to it, is framed with a double reveal and covered with trowelled Venetian plaster, which contrasts with the plain matte finish on the other white walls. A wall of built-in closets sheathed with quarter-sawn, horizontally oriented, white oak veneer separates the bedrooms.

The new long wall that separates the living spaces from the services is made of fibreboard covered with a shiny dark-brown lacquer finish. Since this had to be sprayed on in the factory, the wall had to be removed after it was built on site and then re-installed after the surface was applied – no easy trick since there was no protruding hardware. The architect-contractors used vacuum clips like those employed to install large sheets of glass. The wall stands on a grid of 61 x 61-centimetre (24 x 24-inch) French limestone tiles with a slight reveal that makes it appear to float. The stainless-steel refrigerator is tucked into it (other kitchen appliances line the inner wall that separates the apartment from the corridor), as are two handsome bathrooms, back to back with an opaque glass partition between them. The cast-concrete tub in the guest bathroom also frames the shower of the master bathroom on the other side of the opaque glass partition. The kitchen countertops are also cast concrete, as are the ledges over the storage areas under the windows. The degree of consistency in Apartment 25C is extraordinary. The detailing is so minimal and well crafted that it is almost invisible – sensed rather than seen.

MADE not only designed but also built and managed the project from their offices in a windswept, brick, 19th-century industrial building on a pier in Brooklyn where, right behind the studios, is the construction management area with a wall-sized spreadsheet and the well-equipped factory, so the architects can quickly and easily go back and forth, refining and sometimes even redesigning projects already under way. The factory has a big table saw, a cross-cut saw, an edge bander for taping plywood, a drum sander for smoothing out wide things (such as cabinet door faces) a planer and a joiner, all of which coexist with a central dust collector that removes sawdust from each machine. And there is a lot of storage for efficient organisation.

'I think making things well is more about knowledge and information and *planning* than anything else,' explains Brian Papa. 'Planning, I think, is where contractors fail and where we excel.' According to Oliver Freundlich: 'On our first project, a loft, the contractor took down an existing stair, and six weeks passed before the new staircase arrived.' This was because the contractor did not think ahead. The workmen had to go between floors on wobbly ladders during the entire time the staircase was missing.

By the time they began the 186-square-metre (2,000-square-foot) Close Apartment in 2005, MADE knew how to sequence the stages of a job and had developed considerable technical skill – a good thing

**MADE, Close Apartment, Morton Square, West
Greenwich Village, New York City, 2005**
The southwest corner of the Close Apartment overlooks
the mouth of the Hudson River, the West Side Highway
and Lower Manhattan. The prominent column is
finished in grey skimmed-trowelled concrete.

The third bedroom was transformed into a library that opens to
the living room. One of a pair of Sol Lewitt's wall drawings can
be seen on the right; the coffee table is also by Lewitt.

since one of the clients is a well-known artist. The apartment is on
the top floor of the Morton Square complex in New York City's West
Greenwich Village which occupies an entire city block and contains
condominiums in a 14-storey building that wraps around Morton and
West streets. Rental apartments line Washington Street on the east
side of the block, and a row of new town houses with loft-style
apartments above them runs along Morton Street on the north side.

The complex was designed by Costas Kondylis, a New York
architect popular with developers, and had just been completed when
Leslie and Chuck Close bought the corner penthouse apartment, a
decision based on its superb views of the Hudson River, its proximity
to Chuck's studio, and the garage, which makes it easy for Chuck to
get from his van to the apartment in his wheelchair without going
outside. However, the detailing was poor. MADE needed to adapt the
apartment to Chuck's needs, but the clients also wanted more refined
finishes, built-in storage, a more ordered and less eccentric plan, and
space to accommodate their art collection. The Closes display works
by friends and other artists they admire, but not Chuck's own
oversized portraits. The emphasis in their collection is on portraiture,
though there are two exquisite abstract Sol Lewitt pencil drawings on
the living room walls that flank the gallery.

The living room, with one of the Sol Lewitt wall drawings on the left, opens to the dining room with a portrait by Andy Warhol and provides a view of the kitchen beyond with its Roy Lichtenstein.

A delicately detailed pearwood wall of closets and cabinets lines the north wall of the master bedroom.

When the Closes took occupancy, the apartment had sheetrock walls that met the floor with standard stock skirting boards, the wood floors were stained 'almost orange', and the kitchen and bathroom fixtures were the usual cheap ones developers install to get the Certificate of Occupancy necessary to sell an apartment, knowing most buyers will replace them. MADE decided to bleach the floors and remove the skirting boards. They doubled the sheetrock to make a firmer, more substantial wall surface with a 6-millimetre (0.25-inch) reveal 10 centimetres (4 inches) from the floor – a detail that unifies the whole apartment. They also simplified the plan. However, a long narrow entrance hall (now an art gallery), set at a diagonal to the outer walls, still leads directly to the fantastic view from the corner of the living room, though this remains partially obstructed by a fat column. Since the column could not be removed, the architects decided to articulate it in grey-finish skimmed-trowelled concrete.

The cast-concrete window sills are grey too, as are the Italian basalt kitchen countertops and the 'Close grey' rather traditional, glass-fronted kitchen cabinets (the Closes have had cabinets in a similar colour everywhere they have lived). The entrance-hall art gallery has shallow shelves on which the owners can place their portraits but rearrange them at will. It is an appealingly modest way to display Willem de Kooning drawings, Irving Penn photographs, and paintings by Andy Warhol, Roy Lichtenstein, Alex Katz and numerous other well-known artists.

The architects widened the doorways between the living room and the dining room on the east, and between the living room and a bedroom on the north side, which was transformed into a library. Another small bedroom behind the kitchen doubles as a guest room and Leslie's office. The master bedroom on the northwest corner, facing the Hudson River, has a 4.3-metre (14-foot) long wall of built-in closets and cabinets sheathed in pearwood with a matte finish and a fine horizontal grain.

Leslie's bathroom and dressing room opens into the master bedroom; Chuck's is off the back hall. A pantry fills the space behind the diagonal gallery, and the serious chef's kitchen has a butcher-block table (which doubles as a breakfast area) where Leslie can prepare food while enjoying views of Lower Manhattan, the mouth of the Hudson River and the Statue of Liberty. The kitchen also has two large ovens – large enough to accommodate a three-turkey Thanksgiving dinner – which is rare even in very big houses. The Closes somehow manage to live the American Dream in a supersized way in this apartment, despite their serious work and Chuck's disability. MADE has paved the way here. ⚙+

Shoreditch Roof Apartment

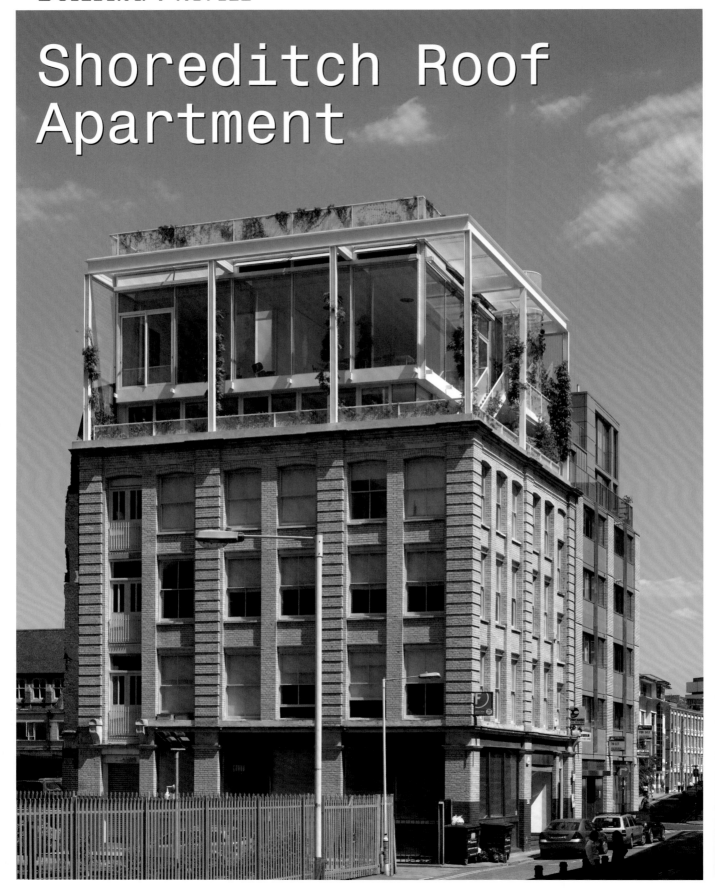

A rooftop apartment in East London is an unlikely setting for a sizable family home. **David Littlefield** describes how the collaboration between Tonkin Liu and Richard Rogers has led to a two-storey addition to an east London warehouse that is thoughtful and sensuous in its spatial planning and detailing, combining bedrooms for four children with unrivalled views.

This eye-catching rooftop development in East London's Shoreditch is, although finished, not quite complete. The architecture is deliberately 'muted', a white and skilfully proportioned skeleton on which nature is invited to play. The clematis and wisteria are as crucial a part of the project as anything else, and architects Tonkin Liu have even put a light above the bathroom skylight – an astonishing 4 metres (13.1 feet) above the floor – in order to illuminate and project the patterns made by raindrops. The more nature works on it, the more complete the project becomes.

For all its clean-cut Modernist elegance, this two-storey home is a place of all the senses, including touch. The fluorescent front door is everything a front door should be – thick, wide and heavy in an almost medieval sense. And the sliding screen that divides the kitchen and main living space from the master bedroom is so robust and massive it is surely bomb proof. Yes, the apartment has a computerised building management system, but the architects (and their client) are to be applauded for not motorising that screen. In an age of flick-of-the-switch convenience, in which anything can become mass-less, it is nice to put your back into something.

Tonkin Liu worked on this project, in association with Richard Rogers over five years. The development is structurally complex but this is nothing compared with the legal wrangling that almost brought the whole thing juddering to a halt on a number of occasions. 'I think it died three times, but each time it came back to life. Each time there was a different stumbling block. For us it was no ordinary architectural journey,' remembers Mike Tonkin.

This is not the place to rehearse in detail the ebbs and flows of the project's genesis – they are easily imagined when one considers the following: access to the apartment is courtesy of a lift in the newer building next door as well as over a bridge that occupies 1 square metre (10.8 square feet) of a neighbour's balcony. In fact, it ever came as a surprise to the owner of the building's roof that the 'air rights' (that is, the space above the surface of the roof) were owned by someone else. For a number of years the project was characterised by a constant round of negotiations and never-ending fees rather than by architectural invention. 'At one point there were seven legal teams working on it,' says Tonkin.

Quite apart from the matter of air rights, the roof of this former warehouse offered further problems – Second World War bomb damage to the centre of the building had been repaired by using

Tonkin Liu and Richard Rogers, Shoreditch Roof Apartment, London, 2002
left: View down towards the entrance, picked out in fluorescent paint. Applied colour is unusual in this development, which was conceived as a neutral backdrop to the inhabitants themselves, similar to the way an art gallery is a backdrop for the works exhibited.

opposite: The two-storey apartment addition to the warehouse building.

The apartment has been configured to make the most of London's changing skyline. Since this image was taken, Foster + Partner's Swiss Re Building has become obscured by a newer building.

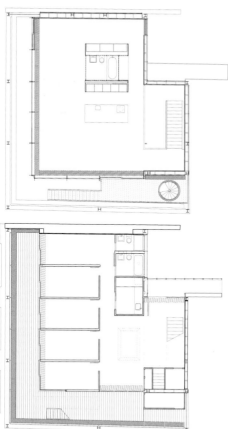

Plans of the lower and upper floors of the apartment. The cellular arrangement of the lower floor contrasts with the more fluid configuration of the upper storey.

columns that were less robust than those they replaced, so the building's perimeter is stronger than its heart. This meant that Tonkin Liu and structural engineers Expedition Engineering had to spread the load of the apartment out to its edges; there are no internal columns and the apartment literally hangs from the frame, which looks like an extrusion of the building below. This frame, this bony structure from which the meat of masonry appears to have fallen, doubles up as a shading device around which vines now creep, providing further summer shading and withering away when winter light is needed.

Much thought has been expended on this little building. There is almost nothing in the apartment about which Mike Tonkin cannot wax lyrical: the four kids' bedrooms, lined up like the cells of La Tourette; the shower head, set so high above the bath that the water feels like tropical rain; the cheap prison mesh (knitted so finely it cannot be climbed) lining the balconies and balustrading; and the care with which spaces are modulated (high spaces, low spaces, expansive vistas, and with views only of the sky). 'It's all about relationships and proportions. Proportion costs you nothing, but it makes a huge difference,' says Tonkin.

So what is it like to live here, in this showcase of ideas? Actually, it is every inch the family home, although many standard domestic features are lent something of a twist. Within the hall the floor drops into a 'conversation pit' from which one can watch television beamed on to a wall from a ceiling-mounted projector. Apart from the lurid front door, colour is provided by the furniture, the planting and all the accoutrements of family life (stickers have been cheekily applied to the steelwork). In fact, during the design phase, Tonkin Liu and the client wrote extensive lists of all the things that would add colour to the whites and greys of the space itself. This is house as canvas, on which life plays.

Planting is an important part of the overall vision for the development. As well as providing additional shading in the summer months, the scents of clematis and wisteria are drawn into the apartment through the underfloor ventilation system.

The west elevation of the development. A spiral staircase leads to a roof garden, where a pair of solar panels is also found – installed to augment the hot-water supply.

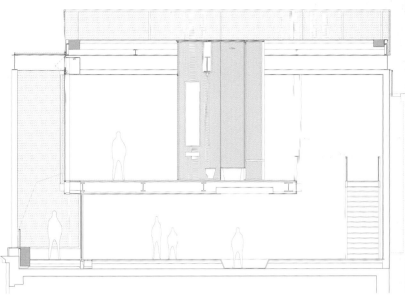

Section through the apartment, highlighting the central position of the double-height bathroom. A skylight in the bathroom is illuminated to emphasise the pattern of raindrops.

The layout is also slightly curious. The four children's bedrooms (plus guest room) are located on the lower floor off the grand hallway, while all other spaces – the living and dining areas, parents' room and family bathroom – are found in the double-height vastness of the upstairs where the views are better. The very un-cellular plan of this upper space is made possible by clustering a wide range of facilities into a central pod, set off-centre, which provides everything from kitchen cupboards (on one side), wardrobes (on the other), the bathroom, a small desk area, a central switching system and the docking mechanism for the large sliding door that cuts the space in two at bedtime. Almost everything is integrated. You would have to look very hard to find an afterthought.

This is not meant to imply that this crisply detailed place is wall-to-wall luxury. It is not. Money has been spent where it had to be: the glazing is almost as big as it gets, while the Corian kitchen worktop must have been far from cheap. And money has been saved where appropriate: the wardrobe doors are from Ikea, while plain lino covers the floor, and polycarbonate lines the walls of the bathroom. It is a project that could not have been achieved without the support of an enlightened and architecturally astute client. For a client of more conservative tastes it could easily have become a place of gadgets and expensive finishes, which is hardly the point of this house. Δ+

David Littlefield is an architectural writer. He has written and edited a number of books, including *Architectural Voices: Listening to Old Buildings*, published by Wiley in October 2007. He is also curating the exhibition 'Unseen Hands: 100 Years of Structural Engineering' which will run at the Victoria & Albert Museum from March to October 2008. He has taught at Chelsea College of Art & Design and the University of Bath.

Jamie Fobert.

JAMIE FOBERT
ARCHITECTS
INSIDE OUT

Konditor & Cook, London, 2007

The architect of several artists' homes, Jamie Fobert is now landing himself a string of acclaimed arts and commercial commissions. From his warehouse in Old Street in London, he explained to **Howard Watson** how the sensitive integrity of his architecture has developed out of 'an inside-out approach', which puts particular store in 'framing light and views' and the sculpting of space aided by physical model-making, rather than the synthetic top-down views that are imposed by widely used CAD programs.

Jamie Fobert Architects (JFA), a small, London-based practice of eight, has long been punching well above its weight in terms of acclaim and awards. Its success has grown out of reinventing domestic environments, including the Anderson House, which won the RIBA Manser Medal for Best House and for which the firm was one of 12 shortlisted for the Stirling Prize. However, the extraordinary architectural integrity of the practice, which seems refreshingly untainted by any desire for sensationalism or showmanship, has also lent itself towards acclaimed – and increasingly high-profile – arts and commercial projects. The key to its success across this diverse range appears to be the application of a rational, topographically responsive aesthetic that is not overburdened by a wish to force through a strident preconception of form. Each project, often at least partially restricted by an existing shell, is designed from the inside to the outside.

Jamie Fobert is a Canadian who studied at the University of Toronto before joining David Chipperfield in London in 1988. He briefly ran Chipperfield's Berlin office and then set up his own London practice in 1996, and it soon became clear from his work that while he may have learnt from the textured, augmented minimalism of his mentor, he is no fawning acolyte. Early residential work included reconfigurations of the homes of the artist couples Antony Gormley/Vicken Parsons and Christopher Le Brun/Charlotte Verity, and underlined Fobert's ability to redefine the parameters of spatial expectation within confined metropolitan housing.

Jamie Fobert Architects is now housed in a curved former warehouse in Old Street which offers several pointers to the way the practice approaches design: for starters, it combines a utilitarian (but far from ordinary) arrangement with an unusual aesthetic despite the restrictions of being contained within existing premises. These elements are found within the Anderson House near Oxford Circus, London, which is perhaps the single building that pushed Fobert to the forefront of residential architecture.

Anderson House, London, 2002
The skylight and window of the RIBA Manser Medal-winning house, sandwiched in a site with no perimeter windows.

The nature of the site forced some radical thinking: the house is inserted into a small space surrounded by 8-metre (26.2-foot) high residential party walls, with street access of only 1 metre (3.3 feet). Without the prospect of perimeter windows, light was obviously going to be a major issue, but JFA approached the complexities by putting forward an elemental solution – treating light as the essential material around which the design would be based. The design came from looking outwards at the site from its centre, envisaging how the building could frame as much light as possible while serving the needs of a domestic environment. The *coup de grâce* is a roof light that forms an angle with a large window, without the interrupt or of frames or joists, giving rise to a surprising perspective. Concrete specially treated to be as reflective and polished as possible, provides both a structural and textural core to the house, forming the kitchen area and stairwell before reaching across the main living area ceiling. Overall, the house, completed in 2002 gives a feeling of light and space on a site that should have been doomed towards claustrophobic darkness.

Fobert emphasises this inside-to-outside approach when revealing a personal bugbear about the thought processes of some other architects: 'I am critical of forms that are only seen from above. Who's going to see these buildings from above?' Usually, before programs such as AutoCAD and PePaKuRa are used, real model-making plays an extremely vital part in JFA's design process.

Tate St Ives extension, Cornwall, 2005–
The current Tate building, with its distinctive circular space, is in the foreground of the model. Immediately behind the curved section, a link runs up the hill towards JFA's new extension. The roof rises into five sections that will provide long strips of glazing, arranged so that natural lighting will not fall directly on to the walls at any point.

Wherever possible, the practice builds at a very large scale of 1:20, to give a true impression of the building. This also allows the models to more realistically reveal the play of light upon the design. The models are taken outside to be photographed in natural light, and are often photographed from within so that the client can perceive the effect of genuine and complex light patterns on the living experience.

It is obvious from the way that Fobert talks about architecture that he has a strong interest in helping prospective architects find the right processes through which to approach design. He taught a design studio at the Architectural Association from 2000 to 2002, became a visiting professor at the University of Lausanne in 2007, and has lectured at a wide variety of universities and colleges across Europe. He says that the most important thing a young practice should focus on is 'Having the right clients to allow your own language to evolve. A strong language of architecture scares the wrong sort of client away.' This is not meant to imply that he forces his ideas upon clients – it is clear that he

often relishes the client–practice relationship – but, rather, that he enjoys working with clients who are receptive to what may appear to be radical resolutions.

The Anderson House has been followed by a string of intriguing residential projects, not least the recent Kander House, a RIBA London Award winner, and the Faha Farmhouse in County Clare, Ireland. The 'strong architectural language' is apparent in both projects, but so is the practice's desire to offer resolutions that are created out of the particular topography of the site and the distinct ambitions of the clients. The Kander House in Hampstead, London, features a striking reconfiguration of a Victorian house into a series of overlapping volumes. The result is an unusual, sleek but textured environment, with much emphasis placed on light and perspectives, which seems wholly appropriate as the client is a successful photographer. By contrast, Fobert is insistent that the Faha residence is called a farmhouse, not a house. It is meant to be completely related to its use as part of a farm dwelling, and the design has to sit among the ruggedness of its immediate surroundings and survive the rigours of a working farm. Fobert was very conscious that neither the clients nor the site would suit 'a slice of chic London stuck in the Irish landscape. It is contemporary. Not slick, though.'

With its long-standing involvement with artistic clients and its original approach towards framing light and views, it is not surprising that JFA has been drawn towards designing art environments. In 2002, the practice was asked to design a sculpture exhibition called 'The Upright Figure' for Tate Modern, and this has been followed by designs for Tate Britain's 'Constable to Delacroix' exhibition in 2003, London's Frieze Art Fair in 2006 and 2007, and the V&A's recent 'Out of the Ordinary: Spectacular Craft' show.

Fobert's best work often seems to come out of the innovative resolution of problems and the design for 'The Upright Figure' was no exception. The life-size sculptures were to be exhibited in the tremendous volume of the 30-metre (98.4-foot) high Turbine Hall so they could easily be diminished by their setting. Two freestanding steel walls introduced both a new scale to the space and a different backdrop, while the figures were grouped on a series of large steel trays, without plinths, so the viewer could address the sculptures at eye level. The scale may be completely different, but this ability to both designate and unify a space through the use of one material and by slicing the volume is directly related to the design of the Anderson and Kander houses. The practice's acute spatial dexterity sometimes transcends typologies.

Following the Tate exhibitions, JFA was awarded commissions for extensions to two high-profile galleries. The design for Kettle's Yard in Cambridge, commissioned in 2004 but pending further financial investment, introduces education facilities, a café and archive space behind the facade of a Victorian terrace. It clearly re-emphasises Fobert's ability to reinvent interior volumes and draw light into restrictive shells. A year later, the practice won the competition to design a major extension to Tate St Ives, which achieves visitor volumes three times those anticipated when the gallery opened in 1993. The project has been delayed, particularly due to concerns

Faha Farmhouse, County Clare, Ireland, 2007
Having created new residences within existing boundaries, Jamie Fobert Architects were presented with a fresh set of residential criteria by the Faha Farmhouse: elevations would have to be considered, as would the view of the exterior from above. The set of buildings was carefully orientated at a slant to open up views of the surrounding countryside. An extension to the existing farmhouse replaced metal barns with Fobert choosing to respond to the agricultural typology with a zinc and timber building. He says, though: 'The internal experience is still the most important. Interior drives the exterior and provides the spatial importance.' The living space steps up the gradient of the hillside and is thereby theatrically raised from the floor level of the entry point. The materials and finishes, such as the black, local Liscannor stone flooring, reflect the rugged west coast setting and the need for the house to withstand non-pristine farming life.

Konditor & Cook, London, 2007

The cake-makers Konditor & Cook hired JFA to design a café and cake shop on the ground floor of Foster + Partners' 'Gherkin' building. Designing within such a building, and dealing with the problems of the curved shape, would put off many architects, but JFA was undaunted and followed its usual practice of allowing an innovative response to grow out of the topography and its restraints. The architects managed to both emphasise the shape of the building and create something independent of it by introducing an unusual mezzanine level above the café area. The mezzanine, which houses the cake-decoration section and kitchen, floats within the 8-metre (26.2-foot) high space and is entirely encased in multiplanar stainless steel, the angles of which make the best use of the curved space. Fobert describes it as taking a rectangular shape and crumpling it to create a new form. Below, the café features block end-grain oak flooring and bespoke black steel and black glass tables, designed by JFA, which are sympathetic to the surrounding Gherkin.

Kettle's Yard, Cambridge, 2004–
Kettle's Yard is a consciously relaxed space for people to enjoy art, rather than a formal gallery or museum. Education is an important part of its remit and a set of Victorian terraces next door have been purchased with a view to creating extended education facilities and a café. While maintaining the original facade, JFA's design will form complex volumes from essentially flat spaces in a new building: a mixture of single- and double-height, highly glazed spaces will create unusual perspectives while drawing a great deal of necessary light into the building. The children's education room glazed from both the street and the lobby, will be on the ground floor and will rise up through the next level, while the first-floor café will be pulled back and glazed to provide views over the main volume. The client was given confidence by what JFA managed to achieve behind the Victorian facade of the Kander House.

that the new building will lead to the loss of a set of permit-holders' parking bays, but hopefully the commission will give the practice the chance to show that the integrity of its architectural language carries through to newbuilds on a large scale. Residents may be concerned that a large building among largely residential dwellings will be overbearing, but it is hard to think of another practitioner who will be able to combine innovation with such an intuitive understanding of topography. The roof, serrated with strip lanterns, will be covered with local slate, while the roofline itself does not rise above the surrounding level.

From its inception, the practice has also pursued commercial retail projects. From 1997 to 2005 it designed a series of stores and department store concessions for Aveda, an international company producing organic beauty products. JFA designed three London stores as well as outlets in Aberdeen and Berlin. The remit was to work within existing buildings, with minimum construction. The practice extemporised the very clean image of the brand, which emphasises the nature and purity of its products, through the optimum use of glazing, solid wood tables, stainless steel and polished concrete, which was used for furnishing elements as well as floors and piers. Other commercial projects have been wide ranging, including a bar, office developments and retail, including a Paris store for Givenchy in 2008.

Recently, JFA has designed a cake shop for Konditor & Cook. The practice's ability to work within existing structures was here tested once again, this time because the shop and café was to be housed within Lord Foster's Swiss Re Building at 30 St Mary Axe. Fobert is unfazed by having to relate his ideas to the pre-existing designs of architectural heavyweights – he previously redesigned two floors of a maisonette that already featured a ground floor designed by John Pawson. For Konditor & Cook he drew inspiration from an aspect of his own office design: straight lines are drawn from points of the famous curving exterior to create an angular floating mezzanine level. The resultant design is surprising and adventurous, but refrains from seeking to create conflict with the shell.

Along with Chipperfield, Fobert is aware that too many contemporary architects, and clients, appear to be trying to create ready-made icons, rather than allowing good architecture to speak for itself and be judged by history. Fobert goes a step further: 'We are not looking to innovate. Ever. Innovation in its own right has no interest for me. I am looking to resolve the design of the site – the innovation comes as a way of resolving things.' This is the key to his success: because his buildings are resolved from the inside out, there is a sophisticated, multilayered harmony between the essential purpose of a building, the new aesthetic and the existing environment. He may go on to become famous for ravishing newbuilds, but working through the contortions and restrictions of existing structures has clearly honed an integrity that takes his designs way beyond the sensational or temporary. One can only hope that the protracted negotiations in St Ives and the lack of money for Kettle's Yard do not turn the practice away from the public arena because Fobert could prove to be a master of appropriate urbanism. ∆+

Howard Watson is an author, journalist and editor based in London. He is co-author, with Eleanor Curtis, of the new 2nd edition of *Fashion Retail* (Wiley-Academy, 2007), £34.99. See www.wiley.com. Previous books include *The Design Mix: Bars, Cocktails and Style* (2006), and *Hotel Revolution: 21st-Century Hotel Design* (2005), both also published by Wiley-Academy.

Inhabiting the Body and the Spaces of Interaction

Wearable technologies create a tactile interface with the body of the user, providing a new model for architecture in which the surface between the subject and the object is almost seamless and sensory. As Valentina Croci explores, they also call on us to reconsider a more interdisciplinary mode of designing that accommodates a dynamic social dialogue between highly portable small-scale devices, their remote networks and the physical environment.

Adam Whiton and Yolita Nugent, No-Contact Jacket, 2006
above: The No-Contact Jacket is equipped with an anti-aggression device that can be manually activated in the event of an attack. By pressing a button located near the wrists, the electrified surface of the fabric on the back of the jacket releases an 80,000-volt charge, capable of momentarily paralysing an assailant. The padding and lining of the jacket are insulated to protect the wearer. The jacket underlines the vulnerability of women in an urban context and functions by using the instinctive gestures of the human body.

Valérie Lamontagne, Peaux d'Âne, 2007
below: The Peaux d'Âne suit reflects changes in the sky and in barometric pressure, and climatic variations. The system is composed of a portable device (Weather Davis) that records such environmental variations; a central computer using MAX/msp software that codifies the information; and wireless micro-controllers inserted in the fabric of the suit. Electronic circuits inserted in the fabric interconnect the micro-controllers. The project confers symbolic and narrative value on the experience of the physical environment and underlines the unexplored applications of computational technologies in smart textiles.

Elena Corchero, Solar Vintage, 2007
Solar Vintage is made up of a series of accessories for the
body (a fan, a necklace, a collar and hair clips) in an
evidently obsolete and affected style. The accessories
contain solar cells, LEDs and resistors, rendering them
capable of storing solar energy that can be released at
night by integrated light sources, providing wireless and
entirely ecological illumination.

Wearable technologies are digital or electronic artefacts
that work in close contact with the body of the user. Often
they are related to technological instruments that
reproduce images or music, or Bluetooth technologies for
cellular and wireless connection. They represent a
transposition of the functions of mobile telephones into
objects that we wear, rather than carry in a bag or pocket
as part of a single device. All the same, the primary
difference between wearable technologies and portable
devices such as cellular phones is the type of interaction
between the subject and the object being worn.

Wearable technologies tend to distribute operable
functions to various parts of the body, connecting
activation with performance. In this way a reciprocal
relationship is created between the object and the body to
the point that, on the one hand, the body becomes a
component in the functioning of the device (that is,
activating processes through movement or the variation in
body temperature or heartbeat), and on the other the
object influences the sensorial and perceptive channels of
the user, creating a level of heightened (augmented)
awareness. They are integrated in a discreet manner within
the gestures of the user, transforming his or her methods

of interacting with space and other individuals. As a result of this
potential, we are now witnessing an increased level of experimentation
aimed at investigating new possibilities of perception of the body-
prosthetic and the new dynamics of the user within built space.

Wearable technologies are artificial prostheses for the body.
However, they are not substitutive, nor do they compensate for the
malfunctioning of a sick or otherwise disabled body; on the contrary,
they intensify the senses and perception of the natural body of the
subject's ability to interact with the exterior environment. Similar to
common computer and digital technologies, wearable technologies
allow the subject to recontextualise his or her position, even in
antipodal conditions, in an instantaneous and non-corporeal way,
broadening the spatial confines of his or her actions. The subject thus
acquires a 'diffuse body', a varied presence in the infrastructures of
inhabited space and flows of information – from the space of the body
to that of the urban environment, from direct social relations to long-
distance communication.

Unlike traditional portable technologies, interaction with the device
does not take place through graphic interfaces (the logic of the menu
or icon on a screen), but through tactile and direct contact with the
instruments located on the body. This implies the simultaneous design
of new, tactile interfaces (hand-held and manipulable), and the
dynamics of interaction between the subject and the technological

device. Leah Buechley, for example, introduces digital hardware into body accessories, tying their activation to predetermined physical movements of the user. Seen in this light, the design of the artefacts also implies the definition of the sequence of gestures necessary for the functioning of the device. Tactile interfaces, furthermore, operate using a more emotional and symbolic language. The user's movements must be devoid of any ambiguity – it is necessary to distinguish what is, and is not, related to the functioning of the device – and they must be natural, part of our everyday repertoire of gestures. An example can be found in the No-Contact Jacket, an anti-aggression device developed by Adam Whiton and Yolita Nugent, which is electrified down the back, based on the idea that a hunched-over position is the most common reaction in the event of danger.

The research into wearable technologies reflects both the development of technologies and the social environment in which this takes place (work, free time, holidays, the family, urban dwelling and so on). The wearable nature of the objects affects the perception of distances between individuals, distances that Edward Hall describes as spatial intervals that exist between two bodies, according to the type of relationship (friendship, working relationship, love and so on).[1] These distances are a kind of psychological limit that sanctions the rules of reciprocal contact, based also on the specific conditions of physical space. This is a theme that has been investigated by Teresa Almeida in Space Dress, a dress that can be inflated by the user according to her situation. The dress was originally conceived of for use in the New York subway during rush hour, and thus becomes the material representation of the dynamics of interaction between individuals in a shared space, allowing the wearer to act on her qualitative perception.

Andrea Branzi has pointed out how the widespread introduction of mobile digital and electronic technologies into everyday life has further emphasised the distance between the city as a scenario for fixed architecture and the metropolis as a flow of information, services and goods.[2] What is more, the quality of the urban environment deals primarily with the latter definition. Objects therefore assume a fundamental role in the experience of the city due to their ability to create a network of human relations (immediate or long distance through the 'diffuse body'), the memories connected to a site and the mediation of services. Thus, according to Branzi, it is necessary to refunctionalise the urban context in relation to the new range of objects, hypothesising 'discontinuous' architectural models that are almost situationalist, flexible towards changes in services and relationships between users.

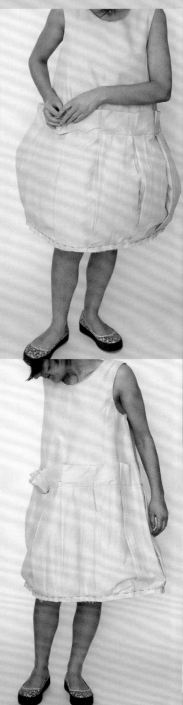

Teresa Almeida, Space Dress, 2006
The dress can be inflated at the push of a button by electrically operated micro-fans, allowing the wearer to physically 'shift' other individuals in overly crowded spaces. The project highlights the need of the user to actively manage her experience of the physical environment, affecting her perception of the quality of space.

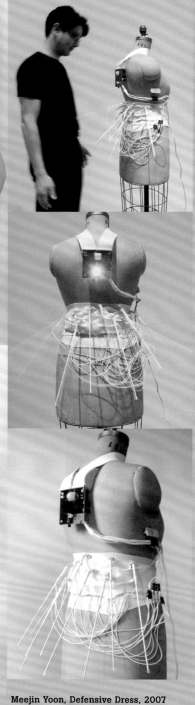

Meejin Yoon, Defensive Dress, 2007
This project lies somewhere between art and design. The suit lifts the prickly feathers the moment the integrated sensor detects the presence of a nearby external body. The feathers are composed of a hollowed copper cable filled with Flexinol, a shape memory alloy. If the external body violates the user-determined safety distance, the sensors activate a small electrical charge that heats the Flexinol, which shrinks the copper and then modifies the form of the feathers.

The design of these wearable technologies must not, in fact, be separated from the physical context in which they are to be used: in other words, together with the object, it is necessary to consider the architectural design of the space and the network of technological infrastructures present in the surrounding and remote environment. Design thus becomes interdisciplinary and context specific: it is necessary to design architecture that is capable of dialoguing with wearable technologies, similar to objects that modulate environmental variables – the emission of sounds, images and smells, or climatic conditions, for example. In analogous terms, mobility, characterised by wearable technologies, imposes that we provide 'smart environments', integrated with digital and sensing technologies, in order to create spaces that are enhanced by interactive functions. We can imagine a space filled with remote-sensing instruments that use electromagnetic waves or fields, computers immersed in space (for example, ubicomp and pervasive computing), and devices that are integrated in physical objects.

Many projects, such as Solar Vintage by Elena Corchero, analyse the way users move in a space, and address problems such as the self-sufficiency of worn technological systems. Corchero's devices are capable of storing energy through solar cells, which can be transferred to other electronic devices, such as laptop computers or mobile phones. These devices can also power light sources or LEDs inserted within the same wearable objects. Wearable technologies therefore transform the way the user perceives a space, underlining his or her active role in experiencing environments and services.

The interaction between wearable objects and built space thus places emphasis on the fruition of the man-made (built) environment, and on the social dynamics that take place within it. The body and the emotional and sensorial dimensions must be at the centre of design in order to generate new, even more experimental topics for more interdisciplinary and user-focused architectural design. Δ+

Translated from the Italian version into English by Paul David Blackmore.

Valentina Croci is a freelance journalist of industrial design and architecture. She graduated from Venice University of Architecture (IUAV), and attained an MSc in architectural history from the Bartlett School of Architecture, London. She achieved a PhD in industrial design sciences at the IUAV with a theoretical thesis on wearable digital technologies.

Notes
1. Edward Hall, *The Hidden Dimension*, Doubleday (New York), 1966.
2. Andrea Branzi, *Modernità debole e diffusa. IL mondo del progetto all'inizio del XXI secolo*, Skira (Milan), 2006.

Leah Buechley, Lilypad Arduino, 2007
Leah Buechley uses form to investigate alternatives to electronic interfaces. Lilypad Arduino incorporates Arduino hardware within fabric pads 6.3 centimetre (2.5 inches) in diameter, which are interconnected by micro-controllers and electrical circuits. During a performance in collaboration with Michael Theodore, the user wore a sweater equipped with sensing appendages capable of monitoring muscular movement, acceleration and direct contact with the wearable device. The data were detected by an external computer allowing changes in sound or other output in the room according to the movement of the user.

Jenny Chowdhury, 802.11 Apparel, 2007
This series of clothing interacts with the movement of the wearer. Each garment features five strips of fabric with integrated electrical circuits, sensors/detectors and WI-FI signals, Arduino micro-controllers and LEDs. The garments emit light dependent on the movements of the wearer and variations in the electromagnetic fields in the environment, providing a means of visualising both interaction with, and the exchange of energy within, a space.

Can Architectural Design Be Research?
Fabricating Complexity

In the second part of this mini 'Unit Factor' series on design as research (see previous article in *AD*, Vol 78, No 3, 2008), **Michael Weinstock** turns his attention to fabrication. He explores this through the pioneering work of designtoproduction, a firm who have made it their business to realise complexity in architecture.

The Alpenzoo Station during construction.

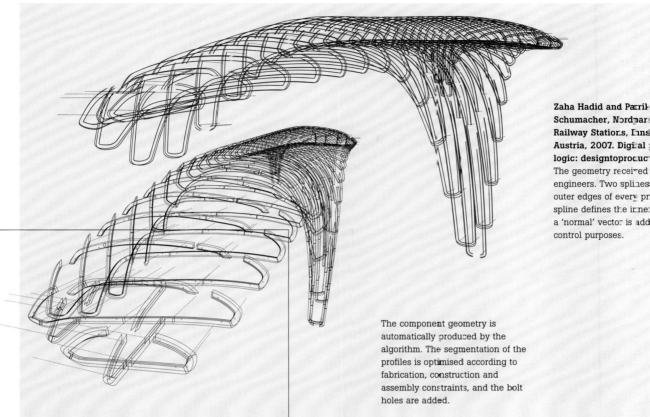

Zaha Hadid and Patrik Schumacher, Nordpark Cable Railway Stations, Innsbruck, Austria, 2007. Digital production logic: designtoproduction
The geometry received from the engineers. Two splines define the outer edges of every profile, a third spline defines the inner edge, and a 'normal' vector is added for control purposes.

The component geometry is automatically produced by the algorithm. The segmentation of the profiles is optimised according to fabrication, construction and assembly constraints, and the bolt holes are added.

If architectural research is possible, it tends to proceed by incremental advances in a series of realised experiments. Experimental designs may indeed produce new and complex forms, but they have to be realised within the general context of established material production systems. The materialisation of complex forms is the focus of the new multidisciplinary practice designtoproduction. The configuration of the practice is orientated towards digital manufacturing: Fabian Scheurer is a computer scientist, and his two partners Christoph Schindler and Arnold Walz are architects with much experience in the fields of parametrics and process engineering. In the two years since they joined forces, they have designed the production logic for Zaha Hadid's Nordpark Cable Railway Stations (Innsbruck, Austria, 2006), Renzo Piano's Zentrum Paul Klee (Berne, Switzerland, 2005), Daniel Libeskind's *Futuropolis* wooden structure (St Gallen, Switzerland, 2005), UNStudio's Mercedes Benz Museum (Stuttgart, Germany, 2006) and the EPFL Learning Centre now being built in Lausanne, Switzerland, by SANAA.

Creating complex forms from standard materials requires that the information, or complexity, must flow along the production chain. Fabian Scheurer explains that designtoproduction's use of the word 'complexity' does not so much refer to the complications of the geometry but is used in the context of information theory to describe the amount of information that is embedded in a system and its components. If all the components are simple and similar, for example standard bricks, then there is no complexity in the components, and complexity lies instead in the sequence and pattern of assembly on site. The information that resides in the brick is the material property and dimension, and the information that the mason adds to the system is the order, position and orientation in space. Altering the order and pattern of assembly away from standard bond patterns adds complexity. And if more complicated building blocks are fabricated, some of the complexity is shifted from the assembly to the component and time on site is saved.

Another way to add information is to gradually alter the shape of the individual components, as was the case in designtoproduction's Inventioneering Architecture project. This was a 40-metre (131.2-foot) long exhibition platform, double curved with varying heights up to 1.5 metres (4.9 feet). The practice was supplied with a digital model and 1:50 model, their task being to find the manufacturing method. A CNC router would machine the model in about an hour, depending on the material and size of the tool used. However, it was always clear that a different approach would be needed for the full-scale object as it is 50 times larger, requiring 50 x 50 x 50 more material to be removed, which would have required 125,000 machine hours, or 14 years and 3 months.

The practice's solution was to cut the platform into 1,000 sections, each 40 millimetres (1.57 inches) wide, cut from flat MDF boards with a five-axis CNC router and then mounted side by side. By rotating the cutting tool around its axis of movement, the upper side of each section became a ruled surface that followed the curvature of the platform in both directions. The key to the process was a set of scripts written within a standard CAD system. The first script imported the NURBS surface from the original digital model and generated sections at 40-millimetre (1.57-inch) intervals, and a second script translated the information (coordinates and angles) into the tool paths for cutting and the drilling locations for the dowels. A third script arranged and optimised the individual members on the MDF boards and generated the machine code for the five-axis CNC router. The information was thus embedded in the individual shape of every single component, and its individual numerical address in the overall form. The effort required to assemble the final structure was very low, as each piece just snapped into place.

What Scheurer and his partners call an 'adaptive building system' is a system of parametric components that are proliferated over a form and are adapted to the local geometry. The digital production chain ensures that information travels from design to production and that the geometrical information is completely embedded into the components so that they fit only in one place and so define the geometry for their neighbouring components. An excellent example is designtoproduction's work on the double-curved glass roofs of Zaha Hadid's Nordpark Cable Railway Stations in Innsbruck, Austria. The railway comprises four stations (Congress, Löwenhaus, Alpenzoo and Hungerburg), two 34-metre (111.5-foot) pylons and a steel cable stayed suspension bridge spanning the River Inn.

Once a manufacturing method had been established for the glass panels, each uniquely shaped, and an appropriate construction method developed for the load-bearing steel structure, the way in which they were to be joined was considered. The usual method would be to design and make metal adjustable joints, an expensive process that also requires every single joint to be adjusted before the panels are mounted, resulting in extensive measuring and fine tuning during the assembly process.

The solution used an inexpensive material which was simple to manufacture, and required no on-site adjustment. Individual profiles, each cut from polyethylene boards to its own specific angle, sit on the steel support ribs, and metal strips are glued to the glass panels and fixed to the profiles with simple screws. The geometry of the profiles was defined as spline-curves in a CAD model, and scripts were written to automate the production of the profiles, the placement of drill holes, the nesting of the profiles for the most economical use of the material in cutting, and the generation of the machine code for the five-axis CNC router. A unique identification code was also automatically generated for each component. More than 2,500 individually shaped parts were prefabricated, each fitting at the correct angle without further adjustments.

The new EPFL Learning Centre by SANAA in Lausanne, Switzerland, is being constructed with an enormous concrete slab of 20,000 square metres (215,278 square feet) that smoothly undulates up and down, with a more than 6.5 metre (21.3 foot) height variation. Reinforced concrete can be cast into almost any shape, but standard formwork systems cannot produce double-curved surfaces. The solution, developed by the general contractor, the engineering consultants and the formwork contractor, was to combine a standard table system with custom extensions. On a grid of 2.5 x 2.5 metres (8.2 x 8.2 feet), scaffolding is erected to a height just below the intended concrete surface. The remaining space is filled by a wooden box that is custom-built for every grid cell. The box is covered with a sheet of plywood, forced to the exact curvature by screwing it to six or seven vertical cleats, each individually cut from plywood. Scale effects are critical – the double-curved portion of the slab has an area of 7,500 square metres (80,729 square feet). This area is divided into

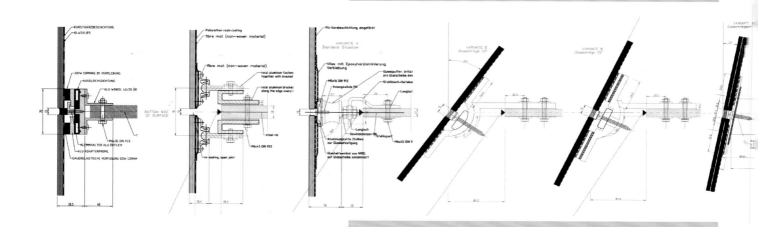

1,458 tables, making a total of 9,744 cleats, each of which is uniquely shaped and has to be designed and fabricated individually. Controlling the logistics is crucial to ensure that each component is situated correctly, and the flow of information has to be designed, as every extra minute needed to build a cleat adds up to an extra man-month of work when it is repeated 10,000 times over.

Designtoproduction is a practice that is uniquely located in an area that simply did not exist a decade ago, working between architects, engineers and fabricators. It is founded on the understanding that all architectural forms are constructed from components that have to be created from standard materials that are usually supplied as either straight beams or flat sheets. Even 'formless' materials, such as concrete, require formwork that has to be built up from standard materials. All non-standard or experimental forms require an enormous amount of information to describe them. The complexity is irreducible, so the aim is to transfer it down the production chain as smoothly as possible. The design effort shifts from describing the overall geometry to creating and handling the information of production. For new and experimental practices, the impact of such work is clear: generating the parameters of digital production can be accomplished post design, but incorporating them as inputs to the design process will optimise experimental designs for economic production. Expertise in this area guarantees the material realisation of experimental designs. ∆+

'Unit Factor' is edited by Michael Weinstock, who is Academic Head and Master of Technical Studies at the Architectural Association School of Architecture in London. He is co-guest-editor with Michael Hensel and Achim Menges of the *Emergence: Morphogenetic Design Strategies* (May 2004) and *Techniques and Technologies in Morphogenetic Design* (March 2006) issues of *Architectural Design*. He is currently writing a book on the architecture of emergence for John Wiley & Sons Ltd.

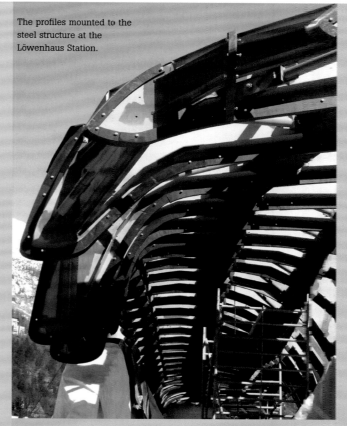

The profiles mounted to the steel structure at the Löwenhaus Station.

Glass panels being mounted to the profiles at the Alpenzoo Station.

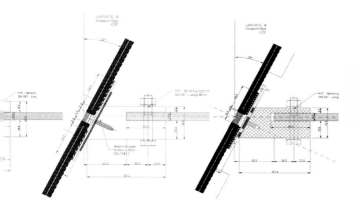

Evolution of the steel-glass joint. Various customised, flexible and adjustable solutions were developed before the mass-customised PE profile was chosen as the best solution.

Radical Experimentation As Research: AVATAR

For four years, AVATAR at the Bartlett School of Architecture at University College London has been advancing the 'digital and visceral terrain'. As its main exponent, Neil Spiller explains how its preoccupations fan out far beyond the merely technological, encompassing the aesthetic, philosophical and the natural, enabling it to question current stylistic tyrannies in architecture.

The Advanced Virtual and Technological Architecture Research (AVATAR) Group (www.avatarlondon.org) was founded, it must be said, by me, in September 2004 at the Bartlett School of Architecture. Its agenda is to explore all manner of digital and visceral terrain, its augmentation and symbiosis. AVATAR also has a dedicated Masters/Phd by Design route for students.

AVATAR is fundamentally interested in research concerning the impact of advanced technology on architectural design. However, it also contributes to discussion on issues such as aesthetics, philosophy and cybernetics.

Technologically, AVATAR concerns itself with virtuality (exploring fully immersed, mixed and augmented environments), time-based new media (film, animation and film theory), and nano- and biotechnology (micro landscapes and architecture, ethics, sustainability and ecology) including reflexive environments and cybernetic systems.

Philosophically and artistically, AVATAR is convinced that new technologies prompt a re-evaluation of

Surrealist spatial protocols and tactics. It also believes that Alfred Jarry's proto-Surrealist poetic pseudo-science of pataphysics and its idea of the clinamen – the swerve (chance) – has great import on what we do. The choreography of digitally enabled chance allows us to create architecture of blossoming possibility where events are fleeting, exceptional and particular.

Narratively and aesthetically, AVATAR considers itself uniquely skilled and positioned to posit new aesthetic systems and codes of representation for architecture, interior design, multimedia design and graphic design.

The most important paradigm shift sustained by new media and technologies, with their consequent ubiquity, is that of the liberation of the user from the stylistic and spatial dictates of aesthetic fascists like architects, politicians and planners. As this century progresses, this tyranny will become

Glen Tomlin, Nested Nanotechture, 2005
Implant location plan. Nanotechnology is used here to record and make visible the nested virtual painting an artist paints, not with a brush, but with other movements of his or her body during the action of painting.

Christian Kerrigan, Growing a ship from a Yew Copse, 2006
Hull section. Kerrigan's project utilised bonsai and nanotechnological notions to harness the growth imperative of trees to create other objects.

less and less legislated. The ability of users to configure spaces that are mnemonic, high and low coded, personal and transmittable is swiftly accelerating. Music appreciation, for example, has become an evolving virtual terrain: music collections can be invisible, remixed, shared, distributed around rooms as invisible but aural graffiti, playlisted to infinite satisfaction. Geotags can be left all around the world to offer insight, polemic, warning and delight. We can make the traces of our lives readable as a new social archaeology. Obviously the great paradox of our age, the prospect of surveillance, always makes us consider the ethics of careful, wise and informationally safe digital space.

In recent years it has become apparent that AVATAR's work needs to explore issues of the performative, the locative, and the harnessing and husbandry of natural architectural systems. Glen Tomlin's research focused on the myriad vectors and spaces, which are never seen nor appreciated, that are generated as a side-effect of the creation of a recognised masterpiece, in this case of Picasso's *Les Demoiselles d'Avignon* (1909). Tomlin used nanotechnological implants located at an artist's wrists, elbows and shoulders, thus as the work was in progress three other nested 'paintings' were generated. The nanotechnological devices simultaneously acted as preventative medical sensors, assessing the health of the user's bone marrow, blood constitution, muscle fibre and nervous system. The project, backed up with extensive technical and medical analysis, revealed a series of architectural spaces that could be provoked, interacted with or used to drive other architectures.

Christian Kerrigan's work is predicated on the fact that putting metal corsets around growing trees encourages the growth of timber that has a higher density and can therefore be used more effectively to construct things. This extreme bonsai technique can utilise other technologies, such as nanotechnology, to create within sections of trees a sort of Purist composition of as yet unseen growing and harvestable objects. In short Kerrigan's project harvests the growth imperative of trees, such as a yew tree copse, to grow a ship, and has a life span of more than 200 years as the copse/ship/launching pier grows – an architecture before an architecture fuelled by the natural power of growth.

Advanced technology brings together many things that have previously been seen as separate and bounded, for example softness and engineering through genetic manipulation. AVATAR is therefore convinced of the value of what Louis Aragon, the Surrealist writer, called the psycho-magical operations of collage. Indeed, collage-orientated thought patterns are often responsible for the creative insight of a project, and allow a designer to think out of the box. The projects illustrated here do just that, and were instigated by such synthetic notions. Architecture is no longer a discrete discipline everything is up for grabs. ∆+

Professor Neil Spiller is Professor of Architecture and Digital Theory and Vice Dean at the Bartlett Faculty of Built Environment, University College London.

Anthropoidal Energy Production
Generating and Harvesting Electricity From Human Power

With the depletion of slavery – large-scale free, if not cheap, manpower – the potential of human force as a major source of energy was forgotten. Here Ken Yeang flags up how some important new research by scientists from universities in Canada and the US has heralded the development of wearable devices that harvest human energy.

The future of green energy may lie in the autonomous harvesting of power from humans. Historically, the Phoenicians whipped their slaves so that they rowed in unison to power ships into battle, and the rajahs in India had human-driven fans powered by servants who stepped and pumped continuously on pedals connected by pulleys and ropes to a series of ceiling-hung parallel horizontal blades. With this in mind, a number of researchers are currently looking into a variety of devices for generating electricity from motion, such as shoes with spring-loaded heels that produce energy as we walk, generators attached to backpacks to harness the energy produced from the packs moving up and down as we travel across the terrain, or the well-known pedalling on a stationary bicycle or walking on a treadmill connected to a generator.

If we can generate energy from the daily movement of humans to power household and work appliances (for example, laptops, iPods, mobile phones and local lighting) and even prosthetic limbs, the accretive accumulation of harvested energy will reduce our overall energy demands on fossil fuels and cut down our reliance on batteries, and will thus contribute to a carbon-free future.

Among a range of wearable devices now being developed is the biomechanical energy harvester, as reported by a team of Canadian and American scientists in the journal *Science*.[1] With minimal effort, the 1.6-kilogram (3.5-pound) knee brace generates electricity from the walking movements of the user and stores the energy as electrical power. Current devices can generate about 5 watts, which is enough to power 10 mobile phones. Running on the spot can generate about 54 watts, and the power production can be doubled if a device is worn on each leg, which also halves the recharge time.

To capture the energy, the brace has a series of gears, a clutch, a generator and a computerised control system that monitors the knee's angle to determine when to engage and disengage the power generation. The design targets a particular stage of the human stride, halfway through the swing of the leg until the foot returns to the ground, and could be extended in future to generate energy from other everyday movements and activities.

Instead of generating energy by creating resistance to movement (which demands additional effort), the knee brace

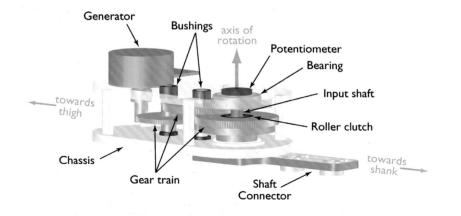

Generator

Bushings

axis of rotation

Potentiometer

Bearing

Input shaft

towards thigh

Roller clutch

Chassis

Gear train

Shaft Connector

towards shank

The chassis contains a gear train converting low velocity and high torque at the knee into high velocity and low torque for the generator, with a one-way roller clutch allowing for selective engagement of the gear train during knee extension only, and no extension during knee flexion.

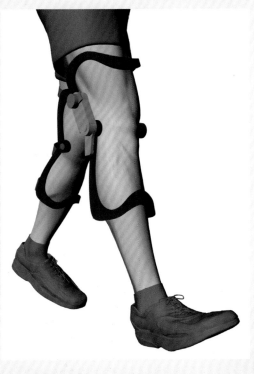

The biomechanical energy harvester comprises an aluminium chassis (shown in green in the diagram) and generator (blue) mounted on a customised orthopaedic knee brace (red), with a total mass of 1.6 kilograms (3.5 pounds).

helps the muscles do their locomotive work by engaging only during the 'braking' phase of the leg's swing, when the leg muscles are acting to decelerate the limb. In doing so it also takes advantage of the 'negative', or energy-absorbing, work naturally performed by human leg muscles during walking, similar to the regenerative brakes found in hybrid cars, where the dissipated energy during braking is captured to drive a generator.

The knee-brace energy harvester operates in two modes:

- Mutualistic mode: currently generates 6 watts with no additional effort, with future versions expected to generate up to 20 watts.

- Parasitic mode: currently generates 27 watts, with future versions expected to generate up to 50 watts for short periods.

Other sources of harvestable ambient energy include waste heat, vibration, electromagnetic waves, wind, flowing water and solar energy. While each of these can be effectively used to power remote sensors, future research places the emphasis on scavenging vibrational energy with piezoelectric materials.

Of course, all such devices are still in their early stages. However, the future may lie in a series of composite smaller and lighter devices that will generate enough energy for each individual to power his or her own daily energy requirements, in the home and at work, thereby providing universal mobility and freeing us from our dependency on the electricity grid. Δ+

Note
1. JM Donelan et al, 'Biomechanical Energy Harvesting: Generating Electricity During Walking with Minimal User Effort', *Science*, Vol 319, No 5864, 8 February 2008, pp 807-10.

Ken Yeang is a director of Llewelyn Davies Yeang in London and TR Hamzah & Yeang, its sister company, in Kuala Lumpur, Malaysia. He is the author of many articles and books on sustainable design, including *Ecodesign: A Manual for Ecological Design* (Wiley-Academy 2006).

McLean's Nuggets

Wireless Power: Out of Thin Air

In this second age of wireless communication it must surely be time to look again at the revolutionary work of Nicola Tesla (1856–1943).[1] Born in Croatia as an ethnic Serb, Tesla was said to have had a photographic memory. In his twenties he moved to the US where he worked for Thomas Edison. Unfortunately, Edison believed that DC (direct current) electricity was the future, whereas Tesla was developing AC (alternating current) as an efficient delivery system for domestic power. Tesla was latterly seen as a victim of the war of currents, although the AC system was eventually adopted worldwide much to Edison's regret.

After leaving the Edison Electric Light Company, Tesla worked as a labourer to fund his research and experimental work on his AC motor and Tesla coils, which he eventually developed in George Westinghouse's Pittsburgh laboratories. He subsequently sold Westinghouse his AC patents and innovations for $1 million, paid off his accumulated debts and began to experiment with wireless power, proposing a system by which electrical energy could be wirelessly transmitted from one location to another. Early experiments in magnetic resonance were said to have illuminated two vacuum tubes at distinct locations in New York City as well as producing some rather alarming audible resonances.

Tesla moved to Colorado Springs to continue his energy transmission experiments, during which, in 1899, he transmitted 100 million volts over a distance of 42 kilometres (26 miles), lighting up a bank of 200 light bulbs, and thus discovering that the resonant frequency of the earth is 8 hertz. He later moved to Wardenclyffe, Long Island, where, with the backing of the JP Morgan bank, he began construction of a 61-metre (200-foot) high energy broadcast tower. However, shortly before its completion, funding was withdrawn and the project was permanently stalled with little public acceptance of it as a viable technology. Tesla was advocating something akin to a broadcastable utility, his wondrous experiments demonstrating how this wireless power (ethereal energy) could be harnessed in unconnected and geographically distinct devices, as if plucking energies out of thin air.

Recently reported by BBC News was the work of an MIT Research team led by Professor Marin Soljacic which has been investigating the potential for wireless power.[2] Inspired by the work of Tesla, the researchers have prototyped and tested a resonance-based wireless energy process that they have called WiTricity. Fitted on to a laptop, a simple coil device, or other devices such as mobile phones, can operate wire free (and potentially battery free) within a WiTricity-enabled environment, while in Japan scientists are set to trial their first commercial wireless electricity experiment by illuminating the Tokyo Tower with 1,200 watts of wireless electricity broadcast from 30 metres (98.4 feet).[3]

Mark Twain in Tesla's laboratory (with Tesla in the background) demonstrating high–voltage electricity being passed through the human body to illuminate a lamp.

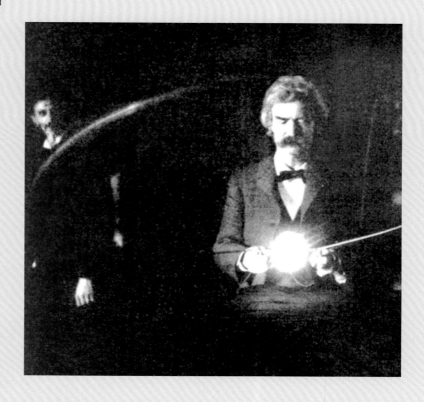

Skip It

Not until every last Victorian house in the UK has been converted, remodelled, altered, modified and up-cycled will the familiar sight of the 'skip' become a memory. The skip is a diminutive relation of the North American 'dumpster', but both, according to Diane Adams, have their roots in the industrial heritage of Manchester.[4] A ubiquitous plate-steel waste receptacle, the skip[5] is said to have derived from the chamfered-sided skep of the textile and mining industries, its contemporary iconic form a relatively recent import from 1960s Germany, which has also given us the building waste-disposal tube and countless other construction civilities. A large builders' skip is designed to contain 6 cubic metres (211 cubic feet) of waste, or, in the case of Professor Marcia Farquhar's recent project, the Open University,[6] an audience of about 25 in what could possibly be described as an urban amphitheatre temporarily sited in a North London street.

We must also not forget the increasingly useful repurposing potential of the part-time leisure pursuits of 'skipping' or its US equivalent – dumpster diving.

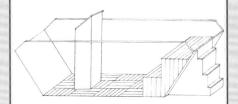

Drawing for Professor Marcia Farquhar's 2007 Open University project – a skip converted into mini auditorium.

No Questions Asked

Before we completely compromise the inhabitants of the modern UK dwelling with water quotas, designated light-bulb types and general carbon guilt, can we not conceive of new and hitherto unimaginable architectures that usefully serve their users and satisfy contemporary and future dwelling desires? These architectures might be loose-fit habitation arrangements or highly organised and highly serviced living machines. There must surely be room for all models? How long can we continue to incorporate any amount of 'lifestyle' compromise in the moribund world of UK domestic architecture? To conform with the Code For Sustainable Homes,[7] a level 6 compliant house must match the thermal performance of the Halley VI research station currently being built to withstand external temperatures of $-30°C$ ($-86°F$) in Antarctica, while draconian controls on water consumption spell the end of the deep-filled full-size bath. It is no surprise that the consequences of such initiatives and legislation seem less than satisfactory, when as designers and clients we continue to ask the wrong questions or no questions at all. Even Prince Charles has had problems with his own eco-home project, to be built at the Building Research Establishment in Watford; it is projected that this natural material based-prototype will be rated at only level 3 or 4, and will not meet level 6, which would classify the house as zero-carbon.[8]

Meanwhile, in the 'commercial sector' formerly known as office design, with slightly more imagination than absolutely none at all, a nascent code for sustainable offices is being devised, with no one daring to ask the question: What actually is the purpose of these joyless peopled boxes? Any number of futile innovations such as 'break out' spaces and other half-baked social Band Aids kid no one that they are working for the man or, to put it another way, what was it about a new office environment/workplace social space that actually needs constructing? The recently interviewed Paul King, chief executive of the UK Green Building Council, does not inspire when describing the 'pulling together of a mult-stakeholder group to … get a richer result and an evidence base for policy'.[9] Making one wonder if there is no end to the proliferation of nest-feathering initiative addicts – or should we not ask? △+

'McLean's Nuggets' is an ongoing technical series inspired by Will McLean and Samantha Hardingham's enthusiasm for back issues of *AD*, as explicitly explored in Hardingham's *AD* issue *The 1970s is Here and Now* (March/April 2005).

Will McLean is joint coordinator of technical studies (with Peter Silver) in the Department of Architecture at the University of Westminster.

Notes

1. www.teslasociety.com.
2. http://newsvote.bbc.co.uk/mpapps/pagetools/print/news.bbc.co.uk/1/hi/technology/3129460.htm.
3. http://www.nextenergynews.com/news1/next-energy-news-tesla-wireless-japan-1.31d.html.
4. Diane Adams, 'Who Invented the Skip?', http://www.manchesterconfidential.co.uk.
5. Katy Attwood, 'The origin of the word "skip"', *THE SKIP*, Issue 7, February 2006, p 5.
6. Ruth Maclennan, *A Manifesto, Polytechnical Institute for the Study of the Expanding Field of Radical Urban Life*, AIR/Byam Shaw School of Art, 2007.
7. http://www.communities.gov.uk/planningandbuilding/buildingregulations/egislationengland wales/codesustainable/.
8. 'Prince's Green Home is Just Too Natural', *Guardian*, 11 February 2008.
9. *Building Design*, Issue 12, November 2007, p 5.

What is Architectural Design?

Launched in 1930, *Architectural Design* is an influential and prestigious architectural publication. With an almost unrivalled reputation worldwide, it is consistently at the forefront of cultural thought and design.

Architectural Design is published bimonthly. Features include:

Main section
The main section of every issue functions as a book and is guest-edited by a leading international expert in the field.

⌂+
The ⌂+ magazine section at the back of every issue includes ongoing series and regular columns.

Truly international in terms of the subjects covered and its contributors, *Architectural Design*:

- focuses on cutting-edge design
- combines the currency and topicality of a newsstand journal with the rigour and production qualities of a book
- is provocative and inspirational, inspiring theoretical, creative and technological advances
- questions the outcomes of technical innovations as well as the far-reaching social, cultural and environmental challenges that present themselves today

How to Subscribe

With 6 issues a year, you can subscribe to ⌂ (either print or online), or buy titles individually.

Subscribe today to receive 6 issues delivered direct to your door!

£198 / US$369   institutional subscription (combined print and online)

£180 / US$335   institutional subscription (print or online)

£110 / US$170   personal rate subscription (print only)

£70 / US$110   student rate subscription (print only)

To subscribe: Tel: +44 (0) 843 828
                Email: cs-journals@wiley.com

To purchase individual titles go to:
        www.wiley.com